LIFE
after
HEAVEN

LIFE
after
HEAVEN

THE MISSING GOSPEL

Rev. Robert Murphy

ARPress
ILLUMINATING IDEAS
EMPOWERING VOICES

ARPress
45 Dan Road Suite 5
Canton, MA 02021

Hotline: 1(888) 821-0229
Fax: 1(508) 545-7580

Ordering Information:
Quantity sales. Special discounts are available on quantity purchases by corporations, associations, and others. For details, contact the publisher at the address above.

Printed in the United States of America.

ISBN-13:   Softcover   979-8-89330-681-1
            eBook   979-8-89330-680-4
            Hardback   979-8-89356-498-3

Library of Congress Control Number: 2024902545

TABLE OF CONTENTS

FOREWORD

I didn't know it then, but I began this book in 1971. I was 33 years old when I picked up the King James Version of the bible off of our coffee table and began my search for direction. Then for me, being a Christian meant believing in God and living by the golden rule. My problem was, too often, as I practiced the golden rule, someone else wound up with the gold. I assumed I must be missing something. So I went to the bible to read the instructions. This was the beginning of my search for truth.

This book presents both my interpretations of scripture and my understanding of my spiritual experiences. The biblical picture of God's salvation provides the framework within which I understand my spiritual journey. This book presents that protion of the gospel that's not being taught or preached in contempary Christianity. Scripture and my experience of God's all-inclusive love is the basis for the all-inclusive hope that this book presents.

I am indebted to countless authors whose works I've read over the last 40 plus years. So many that it's impossible for me to give credit to all of those who've made significant contributions to my understanding. Still I want to thank my professors at the Candler School of Theology at Emory University for teaching me to think theologically. I especially want to acknowledge my debt to several authors whose works have contributed the most to my understanding. John Wesley, Jurgen

Multmann and Dietrich Bonhoeffer in theology. N.T. Wright, Walter Wink, and the New Interpretors Bible in Biblical Interpretation. E.M. Bounds in prayer and the spiritual powers. Most of all I'm grateful for my wife Carole, whose patient endurance and unfailing love enabled us to withstand the storms of life in the ministry. Now after 56 years of marriage, *the two have truly become one.*

Finally I'm grateful for all my readers. I'm looking forward to learning from my critics and all those who respond to this book. For me, writing this book has been a journey with Jesus. The thoughts that miss the mark are mine. Those that express the truth are his. Our web site: brokenvesselsrenewalministries.org provides contact information for those interested in responding to the issues this book raises. All of the Biblical texts were taken from The New Revised Standard Verizon of the bible.

1

You'll Never Walk Alone

W̲e all die. But the often stated notion that "we only live once" isn't true. The truth is there's life after this life. This book is about what heaven holds for you. It's about what awaits you when you graduate from this vale of tears and take your place in glory. This book will reveal God's purpose for preparing a place for you in heaven. It's about what Jesus envisioned for you when he promised, "If I go and prepare a place for you, I will come again and will take you to myself, so that where I am, there you may be also" (John 14:3).

This book is about hope. It's about hope for this life and the next. This book will reveal the hope that has been lost in contemporary Christianity—a hope that has become *missing in action* in the life of the church, the hope that sustained a magnetic joy that conquered the Roman Empire. This book is about God's hope for you. It's about God's purpose in creating this world and the next ... and our place in both. This book is about our future. It's about a future we can count on because it's God's future—a future he has revealed ahead of time and given us eyes to see.

This book is also about the here and now. It's about what's become missing gospel in today's church. Because what you don't know *can* hurt you, this book examines the flawed gospels that have become popular. It highligths the challenges we can expect as we follow our Lord.

This book will surprise you! It may even shock you. There will be times when you will ask, "Why haven't I heard this before now?" There will be answers to that question and insights you will wonder about. This is not a book of fiction. This is a book of truth—God's truth for God's world, truth you can understand. This book is for committed Christians and the curious. Both will better understand God's gospel when the last page is turned.

I'm writing this book for the sake of the truth—truth that I failed to adequately communicate in my forty-one years of ministry in the United Methodist Church. Truth that's taken most of my life to grasp. Truth that people desperately need to hear. Joyous, glorious, breathtaking truth for you and our world.

If we imagine the Christian gospel as a loaf of bread most of us have only been served half a loaf! And much of the missing half is the best half! This book will explore this missing half a slice at a time—all with the hope of bridging the great gulf between the first half, which for many has become old news, and the surprising second half.

This book assumes that millions have reduced the gospel to our receiving Jesus as Savor and Lord in order to go to heaven when we die. Until then we are expected to love God and one another, and do all the good we can. This has become the essence of the gospel for the majority of believers.

It's not that this is wrong. Those who receive Jesus as Savor and Lord do go to heaven. The problem is not with what is said. It's with what is not said. It's with what is missing. This book will be an eye-opener for those who instinctively know that salvation must be about more than this.

Jesus tells us, "We are the salt of the earth"(Matthew 5:13). I will occasionally sprinkle salt taken from my own journey on these pages when there is a good connection with the topic we're considering. One Monday morning early in December of 2012, my heart suddenly flatlined. For a brief moment it stopped and skipped a beat or two, leaving me barely able to hold my head up. I was barely able to speak when it returned to normal. It happened again before the ambulance arrived and drove me to the hospital. I was seventy-five at the time. I fully expected that I would be going to open-heart surgery that day. But God had better plans.

As I lay there in the emergency room, "We have an advocate with the Father, Jesus Christ the righteous" (John 2:1) filled my mind. I've quoted this verse countless times during communion services over my forty-one years of ministry. This time faith filled my heart. I knew those words were true. Jesus Christ is seated at the right hand of the Father, and he is there to be our advocate. With the assurance that sometimes accompanies faith, I simply asked Jesus to ask God to heal me. And I added, "I'm not ready to quit." Immediately I started to feel better. My wife, Carole, arrived in the room in time to hear my prayer. She was the only one in the room with me at that time.

Soon after the doctor returned, and I was off to the X-ray room. After I spent the rest of the day doing the usual tests, the doctor returned and said they couldn't find anything wrong with my heart. His words were; "Your heart is perfect, Mr. Murphy." He went on to name some of the possibilities that might have caused my heart to suddenly stop, hesitate, and then begin beating again. This sudden weakness can be brought on by several things, but other than high stress, nothing he mentioned seemed to fit.

At the first opening I eagerly shared with him what I'd experienced. No skepticism showed in his face. I had the impression that all he has seen has left him with a healthy respect for God's mysterious ways. It's been ten months now since that day in the emergency room, and there's

3

been no sign of that weakness that had me believing that I would soon be moving to the surgical wing.

I'm sharing my ER experience because it breaks through the usual understanding of where Jesus is. One slice of the gospel's missing bread is displayed in this event. Briefly my sense is most people in the mainline churches in the Bible Belt culture of the South think of Jesus as being in heaven with God.

Our church often recites the Apostles' Creed during morning worship. We confess,

> I believe in God the Father Almighty, maker of heaven and earth. And in Jesus Christ his only Son our Lord: who was conceived by the Holy Spirit, born of the Virgin Mary, suffered under Pontius Pilate, was crucified, dead, and buried; the third day he rose from the dead; he ascended into heaven, and sitteth at the right hand of God the Father Almighty; from thence he shall come to judge the quick and the dead. I believe in the Holy Spirit, the holy catholic church, the communion of saints, the forgiveness of sins, the resurrection of the body, and the life everlasting. Amen.

I don't want to be critical of this beautiful creed. But I do want to point out where we are locating Jesus. After his resurrection he ascended into heaven, and now he is sitting at the right hand of God until the day he returns to judge the quick and the dead.

Sunday after Sunday, congregations everywhere stand and repeat the Apostles' Creed, assuming that if they believe these things, they believe the essentials of the faith. When someone passes away, it's often said he or she "has gone to be with Jesus." While that is true, Jesus is often assumed to be in heaven but not with us here on earth. But shouldn't I of all people be celebrating Jesus being seated at the right hand of God as our advocate? Wasn't it from there that he spoke to God the Father and something happened and I went home with a perfect heart? Yes to all of the above! But something more happened that we need to see.

We need to see that he was also there with me, filling my mind with that Scripture that I'd so often read during Holy Communion. He was faithful to this promise, "And remember, I am with you always, even until the end of the age" (Matthew 28:20). Maybe we should start repeating these words of Jesus whenever we confess the Apostles' Creed. We need to celebrate his being with us here and now. We need more than a creed to sustain our journey. We need his Word to keep our balance as we follow him.

It's clearly easier to believe something the church teaches happened to Jesus more than two thousand years ago than it is to believe Jesus is with us today. It's one thing to believe the statements in the creed, something else to know he is really with us. The creed expresses Christian beliefs. Christ with us is a personal relationship. It is, "Christ in you, the hope of glory" (Colossians 1: 27).

Discovering this relationship will bring the peace and joy that countless believers are missing. When he made this discovery, someone once said, "He felt like he was in a desert looking for a camel while riding on a camel." The great *shocking joy* of my life came the moment I realized that *God knows me!* The realization that the Creator of everything knows and loves me filled me with more joy than my heart could contain! That experience brought the realization that he'd always been with me! There had never been a time when he wasn't with me! I'll have more to say about this as we uncover more of the missing gospel.

We could fill pages with verses the authors of Scripture penned proclaiming Jesus' presence with us here and now. But if our resurrected Lord ascended physically (and he did) and "is seated at the right hand of God" (and he is), then how can he also be present with us now?

The answer, of course, is the Holy Spirit. Even though the New Testament never uses the word *trinity* or describes God as three persons, this is implied throughout. God is present with us as the Holy Spirit. Scripture distinguishes God the Father from God the Son ... and both from the Holy Spirit. Yet Scripture equates the Holy Spirit with both God and Jesus. The three are one—one in three persons. This is a great mystery. But if water can also become both ice and steam, maybe we shouldn't be too shocked by almighty God's being three persons yet one God. The doctrine of the trinity was adopted at the Council of Nicea in AD 325 and has been a cornerstone of the Christian faith ever since.

Jesus declared it better that he go away so that "the Advocate," meaning the Holy Spirit, could come. John 16:7 reads, "Nevertheless I tell you the truth: it is to your advantage that I go away, for if I do not go away, the advocate will not come to you; but if I go I will send him to you." Jesus tells them it's better for them to have the Holy Spirit with them than himself! What a shock this had to have been to them, especially given their belief that he was the Messiah, Israel's long-awaited deliverer from the hated Romans, the one who would bring justice and right the wrongs they had suffered for ages. They were depending on him, and now he was telling them he was leaving them!

They must have asked, "How can it possibly be better to have this advocate he's talking about?" They didn't realize that when he was with them, he was limited to being in that one place and time. But when the Holy Spirit would come, he would be with all of them at all times wherever they were. No longer limited by his physical body, in the power of the Holy Spirit he would be with them forever!

Jesus illustrated the relationship the coming of the Holy Spirit would create by comparing it to a grapevine—the vine they were already heavily dependent upon in their daily lives. "I am the vine, you are the branches. Abide in me as I abide in you. If you abide in me, and my words abide in you, ask whatever you wish, and it will be done for you." These verses from John 15 prepared the way for Jesus to declare, "You are my friends if you do what I command you. I do not call you servants any longer, because the servant does not know what the master is doing; but I have called you friends, because I have made known to you everything that I have heard from my Father" (John 15:14–15).

And there's the more familiar verse. "Truly I tell you, just as you did it to one of the least of these who are members of my family, you did it to me" (Matthew 25:40).

Jesus is telling them and us that he is so close to us we couldn't fit a piece of tissue paper between us! He's nearer to us than we are to ourselves! He's closer than our breath. He is so close that whatever we do even to the most insignificant among us, we are doing to him. He is telling us that he is already in us and we are in him! This union relationship is created by the Holy Spirit! When the advocate comes, a new relationship is born. We receive new identities. We are best described as "brothers and sisters of Jesus." We've been adopted into his family. We're part of the body of Christ.

We need to follow Scripture carefully here, lest we run ahead of ourselves. After all, Saint Paul also wrote, "So we are always confident, even though we know that while we are at home in the body we are away from the Lord-for we walk by faith, not by sight" (2 Corinthians 5: 6–7). I admit I am more comfortable with these verses than those that point to our achieving "oneness with him" in this life. For me, realizing this is both earth and heaven's mission!

When doubts come and faith grows weak, I think of Romans 8:38–39. St. Paul comforts me by saying, "For I am convinced that neither death, nor life, nor angels, nor rulers, nor things present, nor things to come, nor powers, nor height, nor depth, nor anything else in all creation, will be able to separate us from the love of God in Christ Jesus our Lord." The truth is that nothing will ever separate us from his love. So we are free to question and doubt. Both have often been my road to truth.

The truth is that it's not that Jesus is in heaven and not here or that he is here and not in heaven. The truth is that the New Testament sees both as true. Both describe the reality. Through the power of the Holy Spirit, we can experience Christ already with us. Our Pentecostal and charismatic friends know this. But I think there are millions for whom the reality of the Holy Spirit and the presence of Jesus with us is missing bread. Once a member of my congregation told me that in the church that he grew up in, the only time he remembered the Holy Spirit being mentioned was when they sang the doxology.

But these are essential truths of the Christian gospel. Apart from the Holy Spirit, there would be no Christians and no church. Paul wrote, "The spirit of God dwells in you." And then added: "Anyone who does not have the Spirit of Christ does not belong to him" (Romans 8:9). The gift of the Holy Spirit is essential gospel bread!

If this is news to you, I hope you will open your Bible and discover the many verses that promise the Holy Spirit to those who seek him. Then believe Scripture! Let God's promises be for you and pray till the Spirit comes. The following words (and persistent prayer) brought the Holy Spirit to me in 1972.

> So I say to you. Ask, and it will be given you: search, and you will find; knock, and the door will be opened for you. For everyone who asks receives, and everyone who searches finds, and for everyone who knocks, the door will be opened. Is there anyone among you who, if your child asks for a fish, will give him a snake instead of a fish? Or if the child asks for an egg will give a scorpion? If you then, who are evil, know how to give good gifts to your children, how much more will the heavenly Father give the Holy Spirit to those who ask him? (Luke 11:9–13)

Any of the following verses might speak to you as well: Proverbs 1:23, John 14:16–17, John 7:38–39, John 16:13, Isaiah 59:23, Ezekiel 36:27, Galatians 3:14, 1 John 2:27, and/or Romans 8:26–27.

To this point we've been considering orthodox Christianity. It's familiar gospel to many, perhaps to most of our readers. Many will feel at home with these basic beliefs.

But for some much of this may come as surprising news. I imagine there are readers in both groups. For the second group this may indeed be a slice of fresh bread. To both groups I say, "The best is yet to come." Having laid this foundation, we can begin to consider that portion of the missing gospel loaf with the most surprising and exciting truths of all.

When I call something missing gospel or missing bread, I'm not implying that anyone intentionally conspired to hide these things. It's mostly due to our only having eyes and ears for the old familiar gospel. It's due to our becoming comfortable with what we've always heard and believed. We've become so comfortable with our answers that we haven't bothered to ask more questions. We've just not felt the need to dig deeper. Sometimes busy pastors have been indifferent to the work of biblical scholars who've labored to bring new understandings to the church. Whatever the cause, that portion of the gospel, which I'm calling the hidden bread, remains tightly wrapped.

None are happier about this than "the spiritual forces of evil" that Paul points to in Ephesians 6:10–17. For Paul, "our struggle is not against enemies of flesh and blood" but against "the wiles of the devil" and "cosmic powers." They operate in hiding but sometimes break out through individuals in places like Newport, Connecticut, or on days like 9/11. But more often they operate in and through institutions like congress where they've helped to create gridlock. They've worked in the shadows to help prevent congress from dealing effectively with critical issues. Where relationships are dominated by the lust for power, and characterized by deception, misinformation, anger, and hate, the demonic is at work. Where Republicans demonize Democrats and Democrats despise Republicans, the powers of darkness govern.

But Satan's preferred institution is the Christian church. This is so because the body of Christ is the greatest threat to Satan's earthly power. Thus, undermining the church is at the top of the demonic to-do list!

There is little openness to this dimension of reality in our mainline Protestant churches. It's difficult to deal with the mystery of the demonic in a way that is faithful to Scripture and tradition, passes the test of reason, and is in keeping with Christian experience. Therefore, the church stays with the familiar. To try to shed light on these demonic corners would take us too far afield at this point. We will leave this for now and press on toward our high calling to explore the good news that's been missing for too long now.

In spite of all its flaws, the church is God's creation, birthed and sustained by the Holy Spirit. Jesus responded to Peter's confession of faith by saying, "And I tell you, you are Peter, and on this rock I will build my church, and the gates of Hades will not prevail against it" (Matthew 16:18). Now more than two thousand years later that tiny band of twelve has grown into a number no one can count. The church really is the body of Christ. God acts in and through the church in ways that he doesn't anywhere else. The church is still God's primary place of grace.

I had just turned eleven when I first experienced his amazing grace in church. After a number of weeks of confirmation classes, the minister asked, "Who is ready to join the church next Sunday?" There were maybe a dozen in the class. One by one they all said they were ready. Since I was seated on the back row, I was the last to be asked. I really didn't feel ready to join the church. I wasn't sure I believed all that I was expected to believe to become a member. But simply because I didn't want to be the only one not joining, I agreed to join along with the others.

The following Sunday I was seated with my parents next to the aisle about four rows from the altar at Wesley Monumental United Methodist Church in Savannah, Georgia. When the choir, ministers, and congregation all stood to sing the doxology, I was struck, overwhelmed even *by the beauty of it all!* I knew then that I wanted to join the church. I belonged in the church. When we were seated, the senior minister called the confirmation class to the altar to be confirmed into the church. Kneeling there, "I accepted my acceptance" (to borrow Paul Tillich's phrase). In his amazing grace God chose me before I chose him. This is my point: The church is God's creation. From the beginning to the end, it's all grace. By his grace I received faith as his gift that Sunday. God continues to work through his church, flawed as it is. Countless souls bear witness to this. In spite of our losing sight of much of the gospel, God remains faithful to his church. In the end, the church's failure to see God's purposes won't prevent his achieving them!

2

THE KINGDOM OF HEAVEN IS AMONG YOU

Where is heaven? This simple question would likely spark a lot of quizzical looks. Some would probably answer, "Up there somewhere." A child might point to the sky and say, "Somewhere behind those clouds." Some might say, "Heaven is a hidden dimension of reality that can't be located." Whatever people think about heaven's location, it's almost always at a distance! It's anywhere but near and certainly not here!

The New Testament paints a different picture. Here's the next surprising slice of our missing bread. Jesus came proclaiming that the kingdom of God was at hand, meaning that heaven had broken into our world with his coming. Mark 1:14–15 reads, "Now after John was arrested, Jesus came to Galilee proclaiming the good news of God, and saying the time is fulfilled, and the kingdom of God has come near; repent, and believe the good news." The great majority of New Testament scholars agree that the breaking in of the kingdom was at the heart of Jesus' preaching and teaching. The kingdom of God and the kingdom of heaven are interchangeable terms pointing to the same reality. In Mark 10 Jesus also equates eternal life with the kingdom of God. By my count, either the kingdom of God or the kingdom of heaven is mentioned 119 times in the synoptic gospels. Numerous times he announced that the kingdom was "at hand" or "had come near." He boldly announced that the kingdom of God was "among them."

The surprising truth is that the kingdom of heaven is with us. Heaven overlaps earth. The kingdom among us is God's project. Jesus promised, "This good news of the kingdom will be proclaimed throughout the world, as a testimony to all the nations; and then the end will come." (Matthew 24:14). The good news is that God is seeking sinners to bring whoever accepts Jesus into his kingdom here and now. *Since the kingdom is wherever Jesus is and Jesus is with us now, then the kingdom is as close to us as our breath!*

The problem is that without realizing it, we've split apart what God has joined together! This is a big slice of our missing bread. God has not changed. Wherever the spirit of Jesus is found, so is the kingdom of heaven! The truth is nothing in all creation can separate Jesus and the kingdom of heaven! It's not that the kingdom of heaven is up there in some distant place. It's simply on a higher plane than our reality. But it is as near as our breath. When we pass away, we won't go flying off to some other place. With our last breath, we'll simply step into the heaven that's already with us!

Granted, his is a hidden kingdom. Like Jesus, heaven is here but out of sight. The presence of the kingdom with Jesus was not perceived by his disciples either. But after the Holy Spirit was given, Paul declared, "He has rescued us from the power of darkness *and transferred us into the kingdom of his beloved son*" (Colossians 1:13). Ephesians 2:6 reads, "And raised us up with him *and seated us with him in the heavenly places in Christ Jesus.*" Obviously Paul was alive when he penned these verses. But he perceived himself as *already in the heavenly dimension with Jesus.* Somehow he was alive in both worlds at the same time.

Few understand that the kingdom of heaven is with us now. Yet there are those who've experienced the curtain pulled back and glimpsed the surrounding beauty of his already present kingdom. It's true that the kingdom of heaven is another stage beyond this life that awaits us when we die. But it's also present with us, and we can enter it now! Contrary to popular belief, we don't have to physically die before we can enter the kingdom of heaven!

Jesus often used parables to communicate the kingdom's presence to his disciples. Matthew 13:44 and 13:45–46 are two shorter parables pointing to the overwhelming joy that comes to those who find the kingdom hidden in this world—so much so that they will sell everything they have to make it their own. They make the point that the presence of Jesus brings the blessing of the kingdom to men now. But only those who "become like little children" enter the present but hidden kingdom (Matthew 18:1–5). To become like a little child means to come to the place of total dependence on God. It is to accept our helplessness to save ourselves and cast ourselves on God. Those who do this Jesus promised to "never cast out" (John 6:37).

More so than the other gospels, the gospel of John emphasizes that "whoever believes has eternal life" (John 6:47). John 5:24 reads, "Very truly, I tell you, anyone who hears my word and believes him who sent me has eternal life." By my count, John's gospel communicates this in one way or another at least fifteen times. Eternal life is life in God's space, the kingdom of heaven.

Being born again is necessary both to become a Christian and to go to heaven for contemporary evangelical Christianity. Jesus saying to Nicodemus, "Very truly, I tell you, no one can see the kingdom of God without being born from above" (John 3:3), is the primary text for this belief. The Greek word *anothen* means "born from above" or "born anew." Nicodemus misunderstands and so asks, "How can anyone be born after having grown old? Can one enter a second time into the mother's womb and be born?"

Jesus answered, "Very truly I tell you no one can enter the kingdom of God without being born of water and Spirit" (John 3:4–5). Jesus then compares the new birth to the wind that blows where it chooses, but we don't know where it comes from or where it goes. He says this is the way it is with everyone who is born of the Holy Spirit.

Astonished, Nicodemus asks, "How can these things be?" Apparently surprised by his question, Jesus answered him, "Are you a teacher of Israel and yet do not understand these things? Very truly, I tell you, we speak of what we know and testify to what we have seen; yet you do not receive our testimony. If I have told you about earthly things and you do not believe, how can you believe if I tell you about heavenly things?" (John 3:9–12).

In this exchange Jesus makes it clear that he is talking about what he has seen on earth! He's talking about earthly things, not about heaven. He's talking about entering the kingdom now, not about going to heaven when we die! He's saying it takes a "new birth by the Spirit" to enter the hidden kingdom of heaven! As a leader, Pharisee, and teacher of Israel, Jesus expected Nicodemus to understand these things, but he didn't. Like Nicodemus, those who are born again apparently rarely perceive the kingdom's presence even if they've already entered it!

When I experienced being born again in 1972, it never entered my mind that I had entered the hidden kingdom of heaven! In my world heaven was universally understood to be beyond this world and was only entered at death. The possibility of entering the kingdom then never occurred to me. All nature was alive and aglow with his Holy Spirit. But I had no idea that I was seeing what Jesus had expected Nicodemus to see—the presence of the kingdom!

I struggled with what my experience meant. An evangelical pastor said it meant I'd become a Christian and I would go to heaven when I died. But I knew I'd become a believer when I joined the church. Another pastor thought I needed to be sure that I was "called to preach" before I went to seminary. I finally decided that I would attend seminary at Emory University for at least a year to help me decide what I was called to do. I was not at all sure that I was doing the right thing when I uprooted my family and we moved to Atlanta.

Finally after forty-one years of ministry I feel I've come to rightly understand my experience. I now believe my experience was more than being born again or a call to the ministry, although it included both. I believe it was also entry into the hidden kingdom of God. For a time I was gifted with seeing something of the present kingdom—the kingdom Jesus was telling Nicodemus he needed to be born again to see! I see this understanding as consistent with the entire New Testament. My experience demonstrates that one can be born again and yet never realize that he or she has already entered the kingdom of heaven! I believe this to be true for the great majority of born-again Christians.

We are not told whether Nicodemus continued to misunderstand or not. But it is clear there's currently an abundance of misunderstanding in our pulpits and pews. Jesus did not say everyone who is born again will recognize the kingdom among us. But Jesus did mean that only those born again can both enter the hidden kingdom now and perceive heaven's presence with us.

John 18: 36 has often been translated to mean, "My Kingdom is not of this world." This has led many to understand the kingdom as being *otherworldly.* The New Revised Standard Version correctly translates this verse as follows: "My Kingdom is not from this world. If my Kingdom were from this world, my followers would be fighting to keep me from being handed over to the Jews." Jesus meant his kingdom had come from heaven. He didn't mean it was somewhere out of this world.

Thankfully our salvation is not dependent on our understanding. "For by grace you have been saved through faith, and this is not your own doing; it is the gift of God" (Ephesians 2: 8). We are saved by grace, not by our experiences of grace. "For God so loved the world that he gave his only son, so that everyone who believes in him may not perish but may have eternal life" (John 3: 16).

There is no need to call for further witnesses. The biblical evidence is overwhelming. Jesus came to establish God's kingdom here on earth. He prayed and taught us to pray, "Thy kingdom come, thy will be done, on earth as it is in heaven." His prayer was answered in part at Pentecost. And because we are children, God has sent the Spirit of his son into our hearts, crying, "Abba Father" (Galatians 4: 6). And along with the spirit of Jesus came the kingdom of heaven, whose nearness he proclaimed. With the coming of the kingdom, God's purpose "to gather up all things in him, things in heaven and things on earth" continues in a new way.

Since the coming of Jesus, the kingdom has become both present and future. It is both already and not yet. The presence of the kingdom is like the dawning of a new day. The darkness begins to slip away before the sun is seen. The future kingdom has invaded our world ahead of its final appearance. Miracles, healing, and the gifts of the Holy Spirit all flow out to us from the kingdom. They are signs that evidence the presence of the kingdom. Hebrews 6:5 sees them as "the powers of the age to come." While Spirit-filled Christians typically experience these things as acts of the Holy Spirit, they rarely understand that these are also signs of the presence of the kingdom of heaven among us.

Believing in the presence of the hidden kingdom means walking by faith, not by sight. For most it means accepting the authority of Scripture over our experience. But it's not in blind faith that we decide to believe this. In addition to Scripture, millions have experienced God's miracles. In every age people have been blessed by the resources of the nearby kingdom of heaven. When Jesus sent out his disciples to "cure the sick, raise the dead, cleanse the lepers, and cast out demons," he said, "As you go, proclaim the good news, the kingdom of heaven has come near" (Matthew 10:7–8). When Jesus told his disciples they were to be "the light of the world" and "the salt of the earth," he envisioned the kingdom of God impacting the world through them (Matthew 5:13–14).

3

A Nation Built in Heaven

The loss of the presence of the kingdom in our Protestant churches is a major cause of the popular gospel being reduced to "believing in Jesus in order to go to heaven when we die." This highly individualized gospel has lost sight of God's primary purpose, which is *to create a holy nation prepared to reign with Christ in the coming new creation!* We debate whether or not our country ought to be nation-building in other countries. All the while *God's building a holy nation in heaven is going on unannounced!* Here is another huge slice of the gospel's missing bread. Who is preaching that God is a "nation builder?" How have we missed seeing this as heaven's great purpose? We'll explore all of this in later chapters.

Since his promise to Abraham that the number of his descendents would be like the stars in the sky (Genesis 15:5), God has chosen a people to bear witness to his works. First Peter 2:9–10 reads, "But you are a chosen race, *a royal priesthood, a holy nation,* God's own people, in order that you may proclaim the mighty acts of him who called you out of darkness into his marvelous light. Once you were not a people but now you are God's people; once you had not received mercy, but now you have received mercy."

Second Corinthians 6:16 reads, "For we are the temple of the living God; as God said, "I will live in them and walk among them, and I will be their God and they shall be my people." These verses and dozens more underscore God's intimacy with the holy nation he's preparing to reign with Jesus in the completed kingdom of God.

Our entry into either the church or the hidden kingdom of God does not bring with it any guarantee of immunity from the terrors and tragedies of life. Jesus didn't promise us financial prosperity or the absence of suffering. He laid many of the evils that torment people at the feet of the Devil. He saw demonic forces as working behind the scenes in opposition to the kingdom of God. Those who respond to the invitation to enter the church or the kingdom enter a war zone. "To stand against the wiles of the devil," we must put on the whole armor of God as St. Paul describes in Ephesians 6.

Evil is more powerful than man. Satan and the cosmic forces of evil are at work both within and outside the church. The kingdom of heaven is breaking into our world, and this is generating a new struggle for world mastery. Although God's final victory is certain, the battle for this world rages on. Satan's highest priority is the destruction of the body of Christ. This conflict brings suffering we can expect to share. When such suffering comes, it can leave those both inside and outside the church with a sense of helplessness. The world may seem hostile or indifferent at best. Seemingly meaningless suffering assaults hope. Where hope dies, despair haunts the walking dead. Souls who lose their hope soon die.

So even if it is present, why should we surrender all to enter this hidden, seemly weak, kingdom of heaven? Why should we "seek first the kingdom" as Jesus taught if it also means being put on Satan's most-wanted list? If going to heaven when I die is my goal, why ask for more trouble now? My answer is for the sake of the biblical vision we've lost sight of and the gospels hidden bread, which this book seeks to unwrap.

First let's look to St. Paul and ask what he saw that we've been missing? Remember that he wrote in Corinthians of "frequent imprisonments, countless floggings, often near death, five times receiving forty lashes minus one, three times beaten with rods, once stoned, three times shipwrecked, in danger from rivers, bandits, my own people and gentiles, danger in the city and the wilderness, often without food, cold and naked" (2 Corinthians 11:23–27). Finally he was beheaded in Rome.

Prior to his death in Romans 8, he wrote of the vision that sustained him through all of this.

> I consider that the sufferings of this present time are not worth comparing with the glory about to be revealed to us. For the creation waits with eager longing for the revealing of the children of God. When we cry abba! Father! It is the spirit of adoption bearing witness with our spirit that we are children of God, and if children, then heirs, heirs of God and joint heirs with Christ-if in fact, we suffer with him so that we may also be glorified with him. For the creation itself will be set free from its bondage to decay and obtain the freedom of the children of God. We know that all things work together for good for those who love God, who are called according to his purpose. For those whom he foreknew he also predestined to be conformed to the image of his Son, in order that he might be the firstborn within a large family. And those whom he called he also justified; and those whom he justified he also glorified. What then are we to say about these things? If God is for us, who is against us? He who did not withhold his own son, but gave him up for all of us, will he not give us everything else?

For Paul there is so much more at stake than our going to heaven when we die! God's purpose in calling us into his church and his kingdom is to make of us a new creation. It is to bring us into that community of grace where the Holy Spirit works to conform us to the image of his Son. It is to complete the work of freeing us from the power of sin, preparing us to become fellow heirs with Christ of all things!

Provided we suffer with him, Paul sees us as heirs with Christ of a world free of sin, death, and evil—a new creation destined to come in fullness with the bodily return of Christ. The new creation will be free from the old bondage to decay and death. The whole cosmos is to share in the freedom of the children of God. "Christ must reign until he has put all his enemies under his feet. The last enemy to be destroyed is death" (1 Corinthians 15:25–26).

The continuing work of the Spirit through the church and the present kingdom is also preparation for the resurrection of our bodies. "For the trumpet will sound, and the dead will be raised imperishable, and we will be changed. For this perishable body must put on imperishability, and this mortal body must put on immortality" (1 Corinthians 15:52–53). "If the Spirit of him who raised Jesus from the dead dwells in you, he who raised Christ from the dead will give life to your mortal bodies also through his Spirit that dwells in you" (Romans 8:11).

This is what our warfare with Satan is all about. Satan does not willingly give up his grip on our world. He has no desire to see the kingdoms of this world become the kingdom of our Christ with you and me as joint heirs. Were it not for the power of the Holy Spirit and the resources of the kingdom, the church would be hard-pressed to survive his attacks.

So how did Paul, who suffered so much at the hands of men and the demonic, understand God to be at work for good in all things for those who love the Lord? He even rejoices in his suffering. He writes, "I am now rejoicing in my suffering for your sake, and in my flesh I am completing what is lacking in Christ's afflictions for the sake of his body, that is, the church" (Colossians 1:24). He sounds this note of his sharing Christ's suffering again in 2 Corinthians 1:5–7 and Philippians 3:10. Paul wants to know Christ both in the power of his resurrection and the sharing of his suffering, "becoming like him in his death if somehow I may attain the resurrection of the dead."

21

Especially in suffering, he keeps his eye on his own resurrection from the dead. No amount of suffering was comparable to his receiving Eternal Life in a resurrected body like his Lord's.

He saw being conformed to the image of Christ as the incomparable good God was working out in all things. He saw that the church must first share in the suffering that comes with the kingdom's presence if it wanted to share in Christ's glory (Romans 8: 17). Peter saw such suffering as evidence of "the Spirit resting on you." In his first letter he wrote, "Beloved, do not be surprised at the fiery ordeal that is taking place among you to test you, as though something strange were happening to you. But rejoice insofar as you are sharing Christ's sufferings, so that you may be glad and shout for joy when his glory is revealed" (1 Peter 4:12–13).

The currently popular prosperity gospel fails to communicate the necessity of suffering if we are to share in the glory of God. There's no cross to carry in this gospel.

The cross has been exchanged for silver and gold. According to this gospel, the Spirit works with those who speak their desires to bring them what they confess. This in spite of Jesus' warning found in Matthew 6:19–21, which reads, "Do not store up for yourselves treasures on earth, where moth and rust consume and where thieves break in and steal; but store up for yourselves treasures in heaven, where neither moth nor rust consumes and where thieves do not break in and steal. For where your treasure is, there your heart will be also." Jesus is saying that idolatry, the serving of other God's, will be the outcome of our getting and keeping as much as we can. Verse 24 reads, "No one can serve two masters; for a slave will either hate the one and love the other, or be devoted to the one and despise the other. You cannot serve God and wealth." There is no middle ground here. We will either serve God or serve ourselves. Worship God or worship the power that having money brings. Serving God leads to eternal life. Serving the self leads to death. The simple truth is that there can only be one number-one priority in our lives!

Life is challenging. For many this must seem like a colossal understatement. Clearly there's no shortage of tragedy and evil in our world. Sooner or later most suffer devastating blows. While there is no fully satisfying answer to the problem of evil, understanding there is a war raging between God's in-breaking kingdom and Satan's hordes can bring meaning where others can find none. Meaningless suffering can become unbearable. This is not meant to imply that this conflict is the cause of all suffering or even most. But it is meant to encourage us to take these seldom taught Scriptures seriously. Our failure to do so leaves the body of Christ blind to the demonic realities that seek our destruction.

4

HEAVEN'S PURPOSE

We hear a lot about our going to heaven but not much about our purpose there. Other than praising God for all eternity, little else is said about what we can expect. No doubt the joy in heaven is beyond description. God is glorified in heaven's unceasing praise. We will never cease to praise Him. God created heaven for this and more. Continuing the work of preparing us for our ministry in the coming new world is a high priority in heaven. In the Scripture often used in funerals, Jesus assures us that "in my Father's house there are many dwelling places. If it were not so would I have told you that I go to prepare a place for you? And if I go and prepare a place for you, I will come again and will take you to myself, so that where I am, there you may be also" (John 14:2–3).

Jesus has already come again in the person of the Holy Spirit and taken us to where he is in the present but hidden kingdom of God. This Scripture points to "dwelling places" beyond this life. It helps me to envision this Scripture as speaking of many rooms, as it's sometimes translated. Because we are so used to hearing this Scripture read at funerals, it's easy to miss that these verses are primarily addressed to the church. If we think about it, being taken to heaven and placed in a room alone would rob us of one of heaven's great joys! Community is our destiny, not isolation! Family and friends will welcome us in a joyous reunion when we meet again there.

So what might we imagine is going on in these rooms? Could it be somewhat akin to what should take place in Sunday school? Classrooms provide boundaries for our experience. Usually we join with others of a similar age. Sunday school and other church groups offer support, fellowship, and learning. Will heaven provide anything less? Of course not! There will be rooms for everyone and every age. There will be rooms for every level of maturity in Christ. Heaven's mission includes our acquiring the mind of Christ. We do not depart this life equally conformed to the image of Christ. Most of us arrive in heaven too wounded and broken to be ready for our ministry in the world to come. Thus, continuing the work of building a holy nation, prepared to inherit the earth, must surely be going on there! It's going on in Spirit-filled community—both in worship and in rooms prepared to meet all our needs and enhance our gifts.

In the beloved thirteenth chapter of 1 Corinthians, Paul wrote, "For now we see in a mirror dimly but then we will see face-to-face. Now I know only in part; then I will know fully even as I have been fully known." Paul anticipates a face-to-face place in heaven for fully learning—a place where the last scales fall from our eyes. "When the partial comes to an end, faith, hope, and love abide, these three, and the greatest of these is love." I believe these three abide both in heaven and the final kingdom in the new creation. Compassion embraces all in heaven's face-to-face community.

I was ten that afternoon just before Easter when I answered the knock at our front door. When I opened the door, I stood face-to-face with the most emaciated beggar I'd ever seen. He mumbled a request for money for food. I asked him to wait there. After I closed the door, I went straight to my piggy bank and emptied it of the money I'd saved since Christmas, which amounted to about ten dollars. I'd been saving to buy a pair of brown and white oxfords I'd seen pictures of in the paper.

Money was in short supply for my parents. They said I would definitely need new shoes by Easter, but I would need to pay for those expensive shoes out of my allowance money. I can still see the astonished look on the beggar's face when I returned and handed him my money. He mumbled his surprised thanks and quickly left. When I closed the door, I knew that I was in trouble. But I also felt that I'd done the right thing. I went to my mother in the kitchen and confessed what I'd done. She was upset and tearful and sat me down and lectured me on the reasons I shouldn't have given away all of my money. I didn't get a spanking or new shoes for Easter. But the feeling I'd done well stayed with me as has the memory of that afternoon.

One day years ago it came to me that I'd be walking the golden streets of heaven in brown and white oxfords. This little story can help us to see more of what awaits us in heaven. Revelation 14:13 reads, "And I heard a voice from heaven saying, 'Write this: Blessed are the dead who from now on die in the Lord.' 'Yes,' says the Spirit, 'they will rest from their labors, for their deeds follow them.'" Somehow our deeds join us in heaven. Or perhaps they are remembered in heaven. The point is that it's in heaven that we see the meaning in acts such as these! In this world the meaning of our lives and deeds is normally hidden from our eyes. It's only in heaven that we discover the treasure our deeds have laid up! They make up the treasures that Jesus said, "Neither mouth or rust consume, or thieves break in and steal" (Matthew 6: 19–21). Heaven reveals the meanings that have remained hidden all of our lives. One of the great joys awaiting us is seeing these things for the first time!

Hebrews 9: 27 declares, "It is appointed for mortals to die once, and after that the judgment." Judgment does not mean condemnation! Romans 8:1 assures us, "There is therefore now no condemnation for those who are in Christ Jesus." The judgment awaiting us after death conveys meaning!

The old gospel hymn "Farther Along," written by Rev. W. B. Stevens, usually brings tears to my eyes. The chorus of this haunting hymn calls us, "Cheer up, my brother, live in the sunshine, we'll understand it all by and by." Heaven is the place we finally come to understand it all!

I anticipate even more heaven's healing! "Farther Along" often awakens tears young and old. They come uninvited with precious memories. They storm my defenses at awkward times. Sometimes I'm made to fumble for my handkerchief in moments of public worship. The oldest tears came with my mother's bipolar suicide when I was eleven. The following year my dad called me in from a baseball game in our front yard. He sat me down on the bed and told me that "he loved my mother too much." After he sent me back to the game, he shot himself in the backyard. Anniversary suicides are not unusual in situations like this. My earlier acceptance experience when I was kneeling at the altar was key in my recognizing these tragedies as theirs, not mine. I'd been given faith and a life to live. I would better understand it all one day.

All of my eighteen aunts and uncles invited me to come live with them, but I chose to live with my grandparents in Washington, Georgia. There I met and fell in love with Carole, my wife of fifty-six years now. My grandparents were saintly Methodist people. I treasure my memories of them. Farther along they'll welcome me again, this time into my heavenly home.

I've led our family's walk to the final resting places of nearly all of my aunts and uncles and two first cousins I grew up with. I long ago lost count of the numerous times I've stood at the graves of church friends and others dear to me. Like so many parents, we've witnessed both of our daughter's families shattered by divorce.

There have been crosses to bear along the way. Some set before us by church members. One by a district superintendent. The heaviest led to the emergence of my own bipolar disorder when I was fifty-six. This followed what amounted to a hostile takeover by another ministry of Covecrest, a retreat/counseling center in the North East Georgia mountains. I'd invested eleven years to rescue Covecrest from financial disaster and develop a meaningful ministry there. Bipolar disorder has generated fresh tears for me and mine over the last twenty years. It has broken though several times, creating more grief for me and my family. I thank God for the miracle of medications that have given me many years of good health. I'm sharing this portion of my personal story so that you will know that I write with a wounded soul. Mine is an ongoing struggle with grief, probably too much to heal in the days I have left. Even though I've already received a great deal of healing, I expect to arrive in heaven a wounded soul. Probably most of us will.

At death, heaven's saints will welcome us into a powerful healing community, the glorified body of Christ—similar to but so much more than the one's described in Corinth and other places in the New Testament. One with heavenly healing for all our brokenness. There "God will wipe away every tear from our eyes" (Revelation 7:17).

In January of 2010 I went to a foot specialist assuming that I had pulled a tendon in my right foot. He prescribed an anti-inflammatory medication and later put me in a walking boot. Six months later the swelling and the pain had only intensified. Carole insisted that I get an MRI, which was finally done in early July. A tumor was discovered in the instep of my foot, which led to a biopsy. The attending pathologist was unable to identify the tissue. He forwarded it to a tumor specialist who agreed that it was not cancer but was unable to say what it was. Thankfully she forwarded a sample to the Mayo Clinic. The head of pathology there identified it as an extremely rare and aggressive angiosarcoma cancerous tumor. By then it had spread throughout my foot, thereby making it necessary to amputate my lower leg and right foot. Thus, I lost my foot but saved my life!

Heaven has rooms for all manner of healing. The New Testament understands miraculous physical healings to be signs. They point to the presence of the kingdom now and toward our complete healing in heaven! Heaven not only restores our souls. There's healing for our bodies as well! I'm going to dance again there! My nickname in high school was "Rubber Legs." Elvis Presley was king in those days. Some thought I copied his moves, but that was not the case. I'm expecting there to be dancing in heaven. I'm expecting to put on my brown and white oxfords and dance for joy!

Heaven will provide all the mental, emotional, spiritual, and physical healing we need. You can be sure this is the case since God has already begun to conform us to the image of Christ and Christ is whole and holy. Heaven's purpose is to complete the healing we've already received in Christ. It is to make us fully whole and holy.

Since God is our and the world's creator, he is able to create and gift us with whatever is needed to complete his purpose. All major faith traditions believe God to be our creator. Scripture declares, "God is love." God's love is a creative love with limitless power. Creation itself displays his awesome power. Creating a new foot for me will not be a problem. His love provides the willingness, and his power provides the means! He puts his power to work in heaven to shape us in the likeness of Christ, and Christ walks on two feet!

First Corinthians 15:47–49 makes this clear. It reads, "The first man was from the earth, a man of dust, the second man is from heaven. As was the man of dust, so are those who are of dust; and as is the man of heaven, so are those who are of heaven. Just as we have borne the image of the man of dust, we will also bear the image of the man of heaven." This takes place in heaven. The mystery of our being recreated in the image of Christ is begun here and continued there. It continues in the heavenly community that's empowered by the creative energies of God.

Heaven is also our place of rest. Hebrews 4:9–11 reads, "So then a Sabbath rest still remains open for the people of God; for those who enter God's rest also cease from their labors as God did from his. Let us therefore make every effort to enter that rest." Hebrews 4:3 declares, "We who have believed enter that rest." Since the kingdom of heaven is present and available, Hebrews calls us to enter now! When we do, we experience "the peace that passes all understanding." Still the Sabbath rest is ceasing from all labor as God did on the seventh day. We only reach that rest in heaven above. While we remain here on earth, there will be labors of one sort or another.

We were created to be cocreators with God. "For we are what he has made us, created in Christ Jesus for good works, which God prepared before hand to be our way of life" (Ephesians 2:10). We often experience great joy in our work. But as we've already seen, there are crosses along the way. Some suffering is certain for those committed to following Jesus. Whether secular or religious, our work is often difficult at best! Entry into God's Sabbath rest means relief from all earthly labors. I cherish the hope of one day entering God's Sabbath rest. There I will "lay down my burdens down by the riverside." I will "lay down my sword and shield," for there will be no more war with the forces of darkness!

Entering our Sabbath rest will bring a profound peace. All fear and anxiety will be left behind. We will rest not only from our labors but from our fears and anxieties as well. As long as we remain "in the body," fear and anxiety "lie close at hand." Even should faith and love be perfected in us, fear and anxiety would remain a breath away.

Both can break in upon us at any moment. Fear is often said to be the opposite of faith. In the midst of high anxiety and fear, people who believe this often blame themselves for their little faith. This is spiritual abuse. Fear is not the opposite of faith. Unbelief is! I accepted an appointment to serve a small church my second year in seminary. Soon after we moved into the tiny parsonage, Carole began having panic attacks. Three times I rushed her to the hospital emergency room when she was convinced she was having a heart attack. The last visit she was told she had suffered a panic attack, but nothing was done about it. This was the beginning of her journey to recover from panic/anxiety disorder. With help and hard work, Carole was able to fully recover.

In 1984, we brought together at Covecrest a team of anxiety disorder therapists, a local psychiatrist, and ourselves, and we began weeklong seminars to equip persons with the understanding and skills necessary for recovery. We continue to offer this specialized ministry through Broken Vessels Renewal Ministries. More information is available on our website brokenvesselsrenewalministries.org.

I mention this in part to say that working with hundreds of suffers has shown me how destructive flawed spiritual beliefs can be. Nearly every person we've worked with has needed to let go of some belief and replace it with truth in order to regain control of their lives. What we believe truly matters! A large slice of the gospel's missing bread is the fact that heaven and earth are not distant, separated realities! They overlap each other! What takes place here is felt in heaven, and what takes place there impacts earth! Thus, Jesus said to his disciples, "Truly I tell you, whatsoever you bind on earth will be bond in heaven, and whatever you loose on earth will be loosed in heaven" (Matthew 18:18).

The book of Revelation is the Bible's great witness to heaven's overlapping nearness. Heaven's curtain is thrown open through the experiences of John. John is ushered into God's throne room by the Holy Spirit. Nineteen of the book's twenty-two chapters tell us what John saw and heard in heaven. Verse after verse describes the worship John experienced. Far more detailed than any other book, Revelation shows us that worship is the heartbeat of heaven! When we arrive there, we will join in heaven's unceasing praise and worship of God! Heaven's soul-shaping worship empowers our being conformed to the image of Christ! Together with family and friends, we'll fall on our faces in worship and rise up healed. Having left this sin-sick, death-dominated, evil-tormented world, we'll worship in spiritual bodies that never die.

Heaven's glorifying beauty will be transforming! John first attempts to describe what he saw there in the fourth chapter. "At once I was in the spirit, and there in heaven stood a throne, with one seated on the throne!" "And the one seated there looks like jasper and carnelian, and around the throne is a rainbow that looks like an emerald. And in front of the throne is something like a sea of glass, like crystal."

The last two chapters picture "the Holy City, Jerusalem, coming down out of heaven from God." Here again John chooses the most beautiful jewels of earth to describe the indescribable beauty awaiting us. He writes of walls built of jasper and a city pure as gold and clear as glass. He pictures the foundation and walls adorned with priceless jewels and gates of pearl. The river of the water of life is bright as crystal.

The most beautiful and exciting of all will be our joining the heavenly host in worship! In the throne room of God, John sees "the Lamb standing," "living creatures," "white robed elders," "thousands and thousands of angels," and more. "After this I looked, and there was a great multitude that no one could count, from every nation, from all tribes and peoples and languages, standing before the throne and before the Lamb, robed in white, with palm branches in their hands. They cried out in loud voice, saying Salvation belongs to our God who is seated on the throne and to the lamb"

(Revelation 7: 9–10). Salvation does indeed belong to our God. *But what is salvation? What is total and complete salvation? How is it described in Scripture?*

5

KINGS AND PRIESTS

Completed salvation is Jesus' prayer, "Thy kingdom come, thy will be done, on earth as in heaven," fully answered! It is the kingdom of God fully established in a new creation as described in the 21st chapter of Revelation! It is "a new heaven and a new earth; for the first heaven and the first earth have passed away." It's when God "makes all things new" and "the home of God is among mortals." It's when there is no more death or mourning or pain, "for the first things have passed away." These verses and more describe completed salvation. *This is the picture of ultimate and final salvation found in Scripture!*

You may have entered the church when you were baptized as an infant, but there is still more for you. You may have received the gift of faith as a child as I did or as an adult, but there is still more for you. You may have been born again, but there's still more for you. You may have received the baptism of the Holy Spirit, but there's still more for you. You may have entered the present but hidden kingdom of heaven, but there is still more for you. And you may go to heaven when you die, but there's still more for you. Heaven is not the end of the story! And neither is hell! *The story of salvation is completed when the kingdom of God is fully come on earth in a newly created cosmos!* The purpose of God to redeem his world though his Son, Jesus Christ, will be completed then.

Until then we remain on our way toward that day. *This is a huge slice of the gospel's missing bread!*

Life is short. There's much greater meaning for me in that statement now that I am seventy-six and not twenty-six. Accepting that is made easier when I recognize that this life is preparing me for something more. This life is like being in kindergarten or at best grammar school. Our life in heaven will be like high school, college, and graduate school rolled into one. There we'll be fully prepared for service in the kingdom of God on earth. We'll have answers for all our questions when the mind of Christ is fully formed in us.

Jesus is working in our world in the power of the Holy Spirit. And the kingdom of heaven is with him wherever he is working. This means we can't limit him in any way. We can't confine him to any church or group. We can't say with certainty who is outside and will remain outside the kingdom of God. To do so is to play God. God is the final judge of the living and the dead and will remain so (Revelation 20:11–15).

Another key expression of the gospel is found in 2 Corinthians 5:17–21. Verse 19 reads, "That is, in Christ God was reconciling the world to himself, not counting their trespasses against them, and entrusting the message of reconciliation to us." The world has already been reconciled to God. Thus, God is free to call anyone anywhere into his kingdom. Now entry into the kingdom of God rests solely on his call and our response. Four verses later Paul writes, "We are putting no obstacle in anyone's way, so that no fault may be found with our ministry" (2 Corinthians 6:3). Limiting the possibility of salvation to a particular church has done just that—put an obstacle in many a pilgrim's way.

We've seen that with the coming of Jesus, the kingdom of God has entered our world. We've seen that those who are born again enter the present but hidden kingdom. We believe that all those who believe in him are received into the kingdom of heaven when they die. We've said that heaven's primary purpose is to prepare a holy nation to inherit the kingdom of God in a newly created world. We've said that the primary purpose for us as individuals is that we be conformed to the image of Christ. This means we become like Jesus in heart and mind. This means we learn to love as Jesus loves. In heaven we will be made perfect in love. We will then be prepared to receive resurrected bodies like Jesus' when he returns.

One of the questions asked when someone is ordained as a United Methodist minister is this: "Do you expect to be made perfect in love in this life?" I answered yes with my fingers crossed. I was not fully convinced that I would attain this lofty goal in this life.

I can say with certainty that I've not reached it so far, and I still doubt that I will. But I do believe I will in heaven. I believe this is heaven's number-one priority for us as individuals. It's only when we've been made perfect in love that we'll be ready to serve in the coming new creation. (We'll look at the use of the word *perfect* later in this book.)

To be made perfect in love is to become a carbon copy of Jesus, who said, "For the Son of Man came not to be served but to serve, and to give his life a ransom for many" (Mark 10:43). Jesus lived this out all the way to the cross. The cross of Jesus shows us what perfect love does. It shows us what it means to be a servant like Jesus. Perfect love is sacrificial love. Perfect love places the needs of others above our own. I doubt very many arrive in heaven already perfected in crosslike love. Neither do I think we are instantly matured in our heavenly Father's likeness upon arrival. I believe being made perfect in love is a process accomplished in the glorified church in the power of our Creator. When we "see face-to-face," our responding in the "faith, hope, and love that abides" will be our part in the maturing process.

Jesus consistently warned against our looking for signs of his coming. He insisted that only God knew when he would return. Many look at all the suffering and evil in this world and think God won't put up with this much longer. But Jesus' return awaits the completion of God's work in heaven and not what takes place on earth. The second coming will occur when heaven's holy nation is completed and made ready, and it's not possible to see any sign of that from earth! Those who see signs of his return in events occurring on earth are deceiving themselves and often others.

We find support for this understanding in Paul's grappling with the question of salvation for the Jews. Romans 11:15 reads, "For if their rejection is the reconciliation of the world, what will their acceptance be but life from the dead!" Paul anticipates the acceptance of the Jews who've rejected Jesus at the coming resurrection.

Romans 11:25–26 reads,

> So that you may not claim to be wiser than you are, brothers and sisters, I want you to understand this mystery: a hardening has come upon part of Israel, *until the full number of the Gentiles has come in.* And so all Israel will be saved; as it is written. Out of Zion will come the Deliverer; he will banish ungodliness from Jacob. And this is my covenant with them, when I take away their sins.

Paul is saying Jesus will return when heaven is filled with the number needed to complete God's holy nation. *The number in heaven and not events on earth will determine the time of Christ's return.* It's likely that there were those in the church at Rome who were claiming to know too much based on signs on earth. They were claiming to be wiser than they were. There's a huge number of people in today's church still seeing signs of Jesus' return in happenings on earth.

The experience of heaven's music was especially powerful for John. Eight times in Revelation he records the words he heard sung. Once he heard, "They sing a new song: 'You are worthy to take the scroll and to open its seals, for you were slaughtered and by your blood you ransomed for God saints from every tribe and language and people and nation; you have made them to be a kingdom of priests serving our God and they will reign on earth'" (Revelation 5:9–10).

Ransomed saints come from every people and nation to reign on earth. They are kings and priests to serve God. We are promised, "To the one who conquers I will give a place with me on my throne, just as I myself conquered and sat down with my Father on his throne" (Revelation 3:12). *There's a throne in our future! We will sit down next to Jesus and rule as kings!* This verse is meant for the completed kingdom of God in the new creation.

Revelation 2:26 reads, "To everyone who conquers and continues to do my work to the end, I will give authority over the nations to rule them with an iron rod, as when clay pots are shattered—even as I also received authority from my Father." Nothing breaks open the heart's defenses as powerfully as the Holy Spirit's love flooding our hearts!

As love-perfected servants, we will be kings and priests! Priests represent God to man and man to God. Perfected in servant love, we will be bears of God to the nations, and we will lead the nations to God!

We are not told who the nations are. It's conceivable that they are chosen out of every nation and religion. Whoever they are, they are not God's holy nation. But Revelation 21:22 pictures them as "walking in the light of the glory of the Lord" in the new Jerusalem, which will come down out of heaven from God. The leaves of the tree of life in the Holy City "are for the healing of the nations" (Revelation 22:2).

Just as pastors distribute the body and blood of our Lord in church, it may be that as God's servants, we will distribute leaves from the tree of life to the nations for their healing. In any event Revelation teaches that when the kingdom of God is established in the new creation, healing becomes possible for the nations. And since God is the decider, that could include anyone. Our reigning with Jesus is for the purpose of our serving the nations! There would be little point in our becoming kings and priests if there were no persons to serve!

Full and complete salvation for us is our becoming kings and priests in the new earthly creation where we "will reign forever and ever!" (Revelation 22: 5). This vision of our destiny is the missing gospel! It has become so foreign in the preaching and teaching of most churches that most have never heard this. The presence of the nations in the coming kingdom of God is found in scripture but is absent in the gospel taught and preached in our churches! Therefore, it is critically important that we ask if other Scriptures support this vision?

God promised Abraham that through him, "all the familes of the earth shall be blessed" (Genesis 12: 3). Genesis 18: 17-18 reads; "The Lord said, "shall I hide from Abraham what I am about to do, seeing that Abraham shall become a great and mighty nation, and all the nations of the earth shall be blessed in him?" Beginning with Abraham's call, scripture declares that God's people will become a mighty nation through whom all the nations of the world will be blessed.

We need to acknowledge that the possibility of God's beginning a new world rests on his being the Creator of this world. If God is powerful enough to create and sustain this world, there is no reason to think he can't create a new world. If his awesome power has only been limited by his choices and promises. If he is truly free to do whatever he chooses when he chooses, then all that remains is for God to act. If this is not the case, then he is not the God of the Bible. Someone has said that God can't make a rock too big for him to pick up. That may be so; however, what I am saying is God is able to do everything that is possible to do, and it's possible for God to bring about a new creation! Granted, such a thing is almost unimaginable! In today's jargon this is mind-blowing! Further along I will argue that this is another good reason for believing it.

For now let's return to the possibility of our becoming kings and priests in the new creation. Since I've maintained that heaven's principle purpose is to prepare us for this role, we need to ask if there is additional scriptural evidence for this.

6

GOD'S PLAN FOR US

The Bible begins with God creating humankind in his likeness and giving them dominion over all creation (Genesis 1:26–27). In the second account of creation, "The Lord God took the man and put him in the garden of Eden to till and keep it" (Genesis 2:15). This verse defines what God intended in giving dominion to humankind.

They were to protect and tend God's creation. Creation was like a garden. A garden can't be dominated. It can only be cared for if it is to be fruitful. Thus, God's purpose for humans at creation is realized when we are enthroned as his kings and priests in his new creation.

Psalm 8 declares we are made "a little lower than God" and have been "crowned with glory and honor" and "given dominion over God's works," and it also declares that God "has put all things under our feet."

Following Moses' leading of the Israelites out of Egypt, God told Moses to say to them, "Now therefore, if you obey my voice and keep my covenant, you shall be my treasured possession out of all peoples. Indeed the whole earth is mine, but you shall be for me a *priestly kingdom and a holy nation*" (Exodus 19:5–6).

The first twenty-six verses of the seventh chapter of the book of Daniel describe a vision that came to him and the words of interpretation that he heard. The twenty-seventh verse concludes the interpretation. It reads, "Thy kingdom and dominion and the greatness of the kingdoms under the whole of heaven shall be given to the people of the holy ones of the most high; their kingdom shall be an everlasting kingdom, and all dominions shall serve and obey them." This verse points to our role as kings in the coming kingdom. Heaven's holy ones end up ruling the world!

We need to always keep in mind that we are to rule as servants! Jesus makes this clear in Mark 10. After James and John went to Jesus and asked that one sit at his right hand and other his left in glory, the other disciples became angry with them. "So Jesus called them and said to them, 'You know that among the Gentiles those whom they recognize as their rulers lord it over them, and their great ones are tyrants over them. But it is not so among you; but whoever wishes to become great among you must be your servant, and whoever wishes to be first among you must be slave of all'" (Mark 10:42–44).

Hebrews 12:25–28 affirms our receiving a new kingdom that cannot be shaken. Second Peter 4 reads, "Come to him a living stone, though rejected by mortals yet chosen and precious in God's sight, and like living stones, let yourself be built into a spiritual house, to be a holy priesthood to offer spiritual sacrifices acceptable to God through Jesus Christ." According to Paul in Romans 4:13, God promised Abraham that he would inherit the whole world. Romans 5:17 reads, "If because of the one man's trespasses, death exercised dominion through that one, much more surely will those who receive the abundance of grace and the free gift of righteousness exercise dominion in life through the one man, Jesus Christ." Jesus famously taught, "Blessed are the meek, for they shall inherit the earth" (Matthew 5: 5). Numerous other verses offer clues that support this vision as our ultimate destiny.

Like an underground river, this vision flows from the beginning to the end of the Bible. We discover it bubbling up springlike in numerous places before it surfaces in Revelation. But for most it remains undetected gospel!

The Westminster Confession of faith declares, "The chief end of man is to know God and enjoy him forever." There is nothing wrong with what is said. The problem is with what is not said. Missing is our scriptural ultimate end—our forever being God's kings and priests in the coming kingdom! It's often been said that God has a plan for your life. Well, he does, and this is it!

As Americans, we believe we are entitled to "life, liberty, and the pursuit of happiness." This is the cornerstone for the American dream. We defend and promote this vision whenever this is needed. God's plan for us is "life, liberty, and a throne!" The cross of Christ displays God's commitment to realize his vision for us. It's often said that freedom is not free. There's always been a price to pay for gaining and maintaining liberty. Realizing God's plan for us cost him the death of his only Son on a Roman cross. Given the price he has already paid, he will no doubt do whatever is necessary to complete his vision for us. Philippians 1:6 reads, "I am confident of this, that the one who began a good work among you will bring it to completion by the day of Jesus Christ."

Saint Paul called our becoming joint heirs with Christ in resurrected bodies in the new creation an unseen hope. Romans 8:24–25 reads, "For in hope we were saved. Now hope that is seen is not hope. For who hopes for what is seen? But if we hope for what we do not see, we wait for it with patience." Paul meant that all of this had not yet come about. This is still true, but now there is a larger sense in which this has become an unseen hope. This vision is generally unseen in today's church. Where can we find people "waiting for this with patience?"

Our inability to grasp God's vision has limited our hope. *Losing sight of the ending of salvation's story means heavens primary purpose also goes unrecognized!*

Seeing both adds to our hope, and hope enables us to live joyously. Hope and joy are closely related. Both help us endure suffering. Where hope dies, joy is buried as well.

Hope that is too small allows both suffering and achievements to become too large. Paul "considered that the sufferings of this present time are not worth comparing with the glory about to be revealed to us" (Romans 8: 18). Lacking this belief, many a pilgrims' faith has crumpled under the weight of significant suffering.

Paul also wrote, "Yet whatever gains I had, these I have come to regard as loss because of Christ. More than that, I regard everything as loss because of the surpassing value of knowing Christ Jesus my Lord. For his sake I have suffered the loss of all things, and I regard them as rubbish, in order that I may gain Christ" (Philippians 3:7–8). Compared to his gospel, Paul saw all he had previously gained as trash. Trusting Scripture's vision for us helps us to rightly value everything else. Jesus asked, "What will it profit them if they gain the whole world but forfeit their life?" We need to ask, "What profit is there for us if we gain it all but forfeit our throne in the kingdom of God?" *The truth is that no amount of suffering or acquiring everything can be compared to our becoming fellow heirs with Christ of all things!*

Paul acknowledged that his resurrection was a future possibility, not a present reality. He wrote,

> Not that I have already obtained this or have already reached the goal; but I press on to make it my own because Christ Jesus has made me his own. Beloved, I do not consider that I have made it my own; but this one thing I do; forgetting what lies behind and straining forward to what lies ahead, I press on toward the goal for the prize of the heavenly call of God in Christ Jesus. (Philippians 3:12–14)

Given all we've seen of Paul's goal, *why have we lost sight of so much of his gospel? Why aren't we straining forward toward the completed salvation the New Testament describes?* Adequately answering these questions would require another book and another author. Still it will help us to understand if we explore a few of the reasons for this.

7

How We Lost Our Way

The early years of the Christian movement saw times of extreme persecution and times of tolerance. Then in 312 the emperor Constantine was converted prior to a decisive battle with the army of Maxentius, a rival for his throne. This led to his making Christianity the favored religion of the Roman Empire. He and his wife were responsible for the construction of numerous churches. Almost overnight the church moved from being tolerated at best to being the most popular religion in the empire. There were economic advantages to be gained by becoming a Christian, so most left the numerous pagan religions and became Christian. Suddenly the church went from meeting in homes or small churches to large cathedral-like structures to accommodate the huge number of worshipers.

The church soon became a large institution with new challenges and opportunities. The church as a dynamic movement, which was characterized by an intimate fellowship with everyone sharing spiritual gifts (such as Paul describes in 1 Corinthians), was replaced by an institutional church with more power given to the bishops.

This enabled the church to deal with critical issues in a more effective way. For example, at that time there were numerous seriously flawed gospels in circulation throughout the empire. Constantine gathered a council of bishops and charged them with identifying the valid gospels to be accepted by the church. They accepted just the four gospels in today's Bible. Acceptance of all the books of the Bible and closing of the cannon was accomplished by later church councils by the fifth century.

Gnosticism had become a serious threat by the time Christianity became the favored religion. This forced later councils and popes to define orthodox belief. Once defined and accepted, the church was able to respond to this and numerous other heretical beliefs that emerged.

Formulating the church's beliefs about Jesus' divinity was another challenge the church soon faced. In AD 325 the council of Nicaea developed the Nicene Creed, which affirmed that Jesus was "of the substance of the father, God of God and light of light; true God of true God; begotten not made, consubstantial with the Father."

These are just three examples of crisis that required the churches attention. They led to crucial decisions by the early institutional church. For centuries now the institutional church has been the chief defender of the faith. Defining and defending the faith has captured much of the church's attention over the centuries. The church has often been a crisis-driven institution. Church history is filled with imposed dangers that demanded the church's full attention. The church has also been a mission-driven institution. Taking the gospel into all the world has been and continues to be a high priority. Much effort has gone into education at every level. Significant resources have gone into the creation of hospitals and other facilities to care for the sick and dying. All of these are good things. When you include them along with regularly occurring crises that required the church to respond and the misguided actions like the crusades the church generated, we can see some of the reasons why a portion of the gospel hasn't received the attention it deserves.

Another key factor has been a psychological one. We live in a death-dominated world. The fear of death contributes to our heightened concern about life after death. The promise of eternal life in heaven helps us face our inevitable death. This supports our focusing on heaven as our goal. When survival is our ultimate concern, so is heaven.

Evangelism has contributed to this issue in ways that have gone unnoticed. Evangelists normally proclaim that if you are saved, you are going to heaven. If not, you're going to hell. Thus, the "if saved" question becomes the crucial one. The *when* and *where* questions are also often asked. If you are saved, you are expected to know when and where you were saved. The *how* question is always stressed. We are saved by repenting of our sins and accepting Jesus as Lord and Savior. When asked the *why* question, people answer that they believe so that they can go to heaven and not hell when they die. There we will be with God for eternity. This is the purpose evangelists typically state for our being saved. Our being saved to prepare us for our role in the coming kingdom is simply not preached. Our becoming members of God's holy nation destined to rule the world with Christ is not proclaimed. Who is preaching and teaching this? *Thus, God's ultimate purpose for us and our world is missing gospel in our churches!*

The biggest reason for heaven becoming the ultimate goal is *God's presence with us now!* God is experienced in countless ways. He continues to draw persons into his church where belief in him is stressed and faith is built. Persons continue to be born again and bear witness to God's love. The gifts of the Holy Spirit continue to be poured out upon his people. Miraculous healing is experienced by many. The presence of deceased loved ones is often felt. Angels acting in crisis situations is experienced and witnessed too. Holy living that glorifies God is emphasized. The presence of the spiritual realm is intuitively sensed by most. All of this and Scripture is convincing evidence of heaven's reality for most.

Abundant evidence for the presence of God means heaven is believable. It is much easier to believe in heaven's reality than the passing away of this world and the coming of a new world. Heaven's reality is much easier to believe than the arrival of a new creation. The church is content with just getting persons into heaven. We humans can usually be counted on to take the easier route to where we want to go. Preaching our future resurrection and role in the kingdom can seem to be counterproductive. Since there can be no experience of the new creation until it arrives, believing this portion of the gospel means believing without experiential evidence. Accepting these things in addition to heaven makes believing harder, not easier. A greater leap of faith is called for, so maybe it's best to let sleeping dogs lie. It's not that the church has intentionally thought about this issue in this way. It's mostly unconscious, not deliberate decision making. When we add this to the other factors we've consider, we can readily understand how and why we've come to be where we are.

Since we live by faith, not by sight, we can never escape the necessity of faith. One of the greatest challenges to belief emerged in the modern world. With the discovery of the phenomenon of projection, Sigmund Freud and others maintained that God is nothing more than a projection of our need for a God. Our need is responsible for our projecting God onto an empty sky. God and heaven amount to nothing more than ourselves projected upward. Of course this is nothing more than an alternative belief. But it's a belief that has persuaded too many.

The possibility that this is the case is undeniable. We need to acknowledge that many may worship a God of their own making. When the existence of God and heaven is set in opposition to this we end up with an unprovable debate. We can point to all the evidence for God's existence and even construct a superior argument, but we have to acknowledge the possibility that we are deceiving ourselves and that a great many people may be creating their own God. This is more likely to be the case with narcissistic persons.

The best argument against this is the missing gospel we've identified. Where can anyone be found projecting a new creation? Who is doing that? Arguing for that is absurd—so much so that it is laughable! The coming of a new world that we govern with the resurrected Christ is nearly inconceivable for those of us who've experienced God. To argue

47

that self-deceived persons are creating and projecting such a thing is ridiculous! The reality is it's been more than the church can do to keep God's vision of our ultimate salvation before us. The fact that all of this is so means that God must be the Creator of this vision. *This could have only come about by revelation! Surely our projection didn't create this! To think so is to deceive ourselves.*

To assert that Scripture was created by self-deceived persons is even more outrageous! Those responsible for spreading the gospel were able to suffer and die in such convincing ways that they turned the world upside down! Their lives demonstrated that it's the world that is out of touch with reality, not them! Self-sacrificing love empowered them to lay down their lives even for their enemies. Death threats did not deter them. They counted it a joy to share the suffering of Jesus. Over the centuries countless believers have followed in their footsteps and made their witness. Dismissing all such people as being self-deceived and projecting a nonexistent God only displays one's prejudice.

Allow me to add this personal note. Should it somehow turn out that my experiences of God have been symptoms of psychosis or self-deceptions, I will remain grateful for them. They have brought me unspeakable joy and hope for tomorrow. They've enabled me to forgive myself and to escape many a temptation. They've been worth more to me than anything this world has to offer! If they have all been self-deception, I wish everyone could suffer the same!

8

MISSING THE MARK

I believe the power of sin is the chief cause of the churches losing sight of God's ultimate salvation. Sin has often been defined as "missing the mark." It's frequently illustrated with an image from archery. Someone with a bow and arrow shoots at a target and misses the bull's-eye. The church has lost sight of the bull's-eye. Heaven as salvation's ultimate goal misses the target. This is evidence of sin as a power working through the institutional church.

The familiar gospel has reduced sin to the attitudes and behaviors of individuals. Forgiveness of our personal sins is the good news of the gospel. While this understanding of sin is accurate in what is said, the problem rests in what is not said. What is missing is again the better understanding. As it stands, this understanding leaves us and the body of Christ missing the mark! This allows sin to become an entirely self-generated reality!

"Sin is failing to give God the glory he deserves" is another more recent definition that implies sin is self-generated. In effect, symptoms (our sins) are the primary cause for our sin. While sinning does lead to more sin, as additions of every sort demonstrate, they are not the cause. Disobedience, rebellion, mistrust, and the like all characterize our part in sin. But there is more to sin than our commissions and omissions.

The most profound understanding of the human condition ever penned is found in Romans 7. There Paul writes that he does not understand his own actions. He sees that he does not do what he wants. He does the very thing he hates! He gives the reason for this in the seventeenth verse. It reads, "But in fact it is no longer I that do it, but sin that dwells within me." In the next verse he acknowledges that "he can will what is right, but that he can't do it." He follows this by saying, "For I do not do the good I want, but the evil I do not want is what I do. Now if I do what I do not want, it is no longer I that do it, but sin that dwells within me." He asks, "Who will rescue me from this body of death?" And then he answers his own question, "Thanks be to God through our Lord Jesus Christ." He concludes, "So then, with my mind I am a slave to the law of God, but with my flesh I am a slave to the law of sin."

Paul sees himself as "mature" (Philippians 3:15). Yet he never claims to have gained total freedom from sin's power. Paul sees himself as a person still struggling with sin. Jesus and Paul are of the same mind. John 8:34 reads, "Jesus answered them, 'Very truly, I tell you, everyone who commits sin is a slave to sin.'" Paul understands sin to be a power that dwells within him. Paul names sin and not himself as the root cause of his sins. Sin is like gravity! It's a power that impacts everyone and everything! Everything in all creation, including the church, groans under this power! Sin is like an ocean undertow, an unseen power that carries us to places we regret.

Imagine your having adopted a small child from some improvised country. When he sees an automobile for the first time he asks; "What is that?"

You answer, "A car. We can ride in it."

He asks, "What makes it go?"

You say that it has a motor.

He says, "I want to see."

So you raise the hood, lift him up, and show him the motor. Sin is like that. It's the hidden engine that empowers our destructive attitudes and behaviors. We start the engine, but once underway sin turns us down the wrong road.

This understanding makes the best sense of my personal experience. The power of sin created the separation from God I endured during my born-again experience. I didn't self-generate this experience. This was something that happened to me, not something I made happen. While I am responsible for responding to the temptations that led to my enslavement, I am not the ultimate cause of sin or death. Both of these powers were present and active in the world before I was born. We're all been born into a world dominated by sin and death. There is no avoiding either one! Paul declares in Romans 3:9 that "all men, both Jew and Greek, are under the power of sin." But there is one who will deliver us from both, Jesus Christ, our Lord!

Musing in the shower one Sunday morning a couple of years ago, I was wondering how any of us could enter heaven if we were sinners. Our having already entered the kingdom does not mean that we no longer sin. Most of us understand that we all sin. Our being saved does not put an end to all our sinning. So if we die as sinners, how is it that we can go directly to heaven? We believe there is no sin in heaven. Sin can't enter there. I wondered if there had to be something like purgatory, where we were cleansed of the last of our sins and made fit for heaven.

While I was pondering this, it came to me that death frees us from sin! Once out of the shower, I went to Romans 6 and read the seventh verse, "For whoever has died is freed from sin." After I read the entire chapter, I saw that freedom from sin's power was achieved by dying. Sin and death (or sin and dying) are intimately connected in nearly every verse. Here when we die to self, the power of sin is broken, and we gain new freedom. At death we will be set free of all sin!

When someone dies, we often give thanks for their "being in a better place." We ought also to celebrate their escape from "this body of sin," as Paul put it. It's not only that they are now in a better place. They are also in a better condition! All sin is gone. They are alive in a place where sin can't reach them. They are totally free from both sin and the possibility of sinning. There can be no more suffering caused by sin! The same needs to be said of death. There will be no more dying for them! The same needs to be said of the demonic, there will be no more oppression or enslavement by the Devil and his agents! Praise the Lord!

My recognition of sin was created by the work of the Holy Spirit. Apart from the Holy Spirit, I would never have realized my bondage to sin. A high priority of the Holy Spirit is to convict us of our sin. Paul realized he didn't create sin's power. Along with the rest of Scripture, he sees sin and death as entering the world with the fall. Both are powers Christ overcame by his death on the cross. Sin is a power that functions similar to my bipolar disorder. It ceases control and drives destructive attitudes and behaviors. Picturing sin in the usual way misses this. This leaves us with an inadequate and partial understanding of the cross. The meaning of the cross for the creation is missed. This emphasizes God's love for us as individuals but says nothing about God's love for the world. In this way we lose sight of the broader meaning of, "For God so loved the world."

Sin and death are intimately related throughout Scripture. They are like two sides of the same coin. All people and all creation are dominated by both. Paul writes: "For the creation waits with eager longing for the revealing of the children of God; for the creation was subjected to futility, not of its own will but by the will of the one who subjected it, in hope that the creation itself will be set free from its bondage to decay and will obtain the freedom of the glory of the children of God" (Romans 8:19–21). Where sin is reduced to our missing the mark, the impact of sin on creation goes unnoticed. The hope that the creation itself will obtain our freedom from sin and death is lost.

Sin as active in the structures of society is also missed. Everywhere sin works to turn us back in on ourselves and away from serving Jesus and others. Sin turns structures and systems of every kind toward protecting the interest of the institutions and away from serving the people. In the political arena party politics becomes a higher priority than the numerous crises facing our country. Sin leads corporations of every size to create policies that become a part of a dehumanizing system. Where rules, policies, and traditions are valued above persons, we become modern Pharisees.

Sin is embedded in every family and every culture. Growing up in the Deep South, I absorbed the prevailing prejudice against blacks that dominated the culture. Sin led most to believe this was just the way things were and the way they ought to remain. Sin enabled this belief to be passed down from generation to generation.

I've witnessed this over and over in my counseling ministry. When I've sensed the presence of an unexamined belief, I've often asked, "When did you come to believe that?" Often the answer is : "I've always believed this." As we explore this further, we discover that it came down from parents, the extended family, or the culture. It really belonged to someone else! Often it props up some destructive dynamic that keeps that person suck in some suffering. Healing and freedom comes when the person asks, "Is this really true?" and considers the options. Even a good belief may sometimes need to be given up and replaced with a better one. An inherited belief really isn't fully ours until we've examined it, considered the possibilities, and freely chosen it for ourselves. Sin works to keep us trapped in flawed beliefs.

Sin is both and inner and outer power, active in every arena of life. Even so, we have a measure of freedom. Ours is a partial, limited freedom. Thus, we remain responsible for our attitudes, decisions, and behaviors.

At the cross Jesus took upon himself the sin of the whole world. The fullness of the power of sin was born by him. Sin and death were put to death at the cross. There Jesus died a real death. Sin flooding his life brought separation from God, leaving Jesus to cry out, "My God, My God, why has thou forsaken me?" (Mark 15: 34).

While we remain in this world, sin, death, and "the wiles of the Devil" will be with us. Jesus told the Samaritan women at the well that "God is spirit, and those who worship him must worship in spirit and truth" (John 4: 23). According to Jesus, both spirit and truth are musts for those who serve God. Many Christians have the spirit but are short on truth. When that's the case, we remain especially vulnerable to the lies of the Devil. Demonic powers and the Devil were not created in the image of God. They are not persons. They are subhuman. Even so, they can make slaves of us. Many just assume they are free. This in a world that the New Testament teaches brings us into bondage to sin and places us at risk to be enslaved by the demonic. The assumption that we are totally free reveals our blindness. If we remain in the dark about this, how will we ever be effective in leading others to the light?

If we only understood that the cross of Jesus was as much about freeing us from the powers of evil as it was about forgiveness of our sins, then we'd give the Devil his due. Our problem is not a new one. Writing to the Galatians, Paul said,

> Formerly, when you did not know God, you were enslaved to beings that by nature are not gods. Now, however, that you have come to know God, or rather be known by God, how can you turn back again to the weak and beggarly elemental spirits? How can you be enslaved by them again? You are observing special days, and months, and seasons, and years. I am afraid my work for you may be wasted. (Galatians 4:8–11)

Paul later described himself as "being in childbirth-like agony until Christ was formed in them." Paul reminded them that they were once slaves of the cosmic powers of evil. And if they returned to the observance of the laws and rituals of Judaism, they would no longer be trusting Jesus alone for their salvation. If that happened, Paul said they would again be enslaved by the demonic powers. They would still be Christians, but they would become forgiven slaves, enslaved once again by the elemental spirits.

Paul described these spirits as "weak and beggarly." They are weak in that they can only acquire and hold power based on lies and deceptions. Their being beggarly may point to their desire to drain Christians of the Holy Spirit's life-giving power. Paul was not writing to a dead church. These were Spirit-filled Christians who in Paul's eyes "were running well." Even so, they were being deceived into believing that they must add obeying the Jewish laws and rituals to secure their place with God. They weren't rejecting the faith. They were seeking to improve it. Paul sees their doing so as idolatry. Their worshiping and serving the elemental spirits would lead to their enslavement by them. We need to ask, "What beside Jesus are we counting on to secure our relationship with God?" Jesus plus good deeds or flawed beliefs that lead us away from following him may set us up to become forgiven slaves, people enslaved again by sin and the demonic. It may be that many have become forgiven slaves.

Our mainline churches rarely consider the work of the elemental spirits. Yet they can lead us into bondage by rejection of the gospel or by behaviors we add to assure us of our salvation ... or through negative thoughts and emotions we harbor. In spite of the gospels portraying Jesus casting out demons on nearly every page, we avoid the subject. This leaves those suffering demonic oppression with little help from the church.

I've occasionally been asked, "Is it possible for a Christian to be possessed by the Devil?" I always answer that I've never encountered anyone I thought was totally possessed by evil. But I do believe this was

55

probably true of Adolf Hitler and other murderous tyrants that have been responsible for much suffering and death. By possession I mean a person who embodies evil to such a degree that all of their attitudes and behaviors are driven by evil. They have lost their freedom to act otherwise. They are fully possessed.

Possession seems to be rare. But I suspect oppression is more common than we think. Evil is such a mystery it's impossible to say what the reality is. I can say I've seen no evidence of possession in Christians. But oppression by demonic powers is another matter. I've worked with persons whose suffering I believe to have been caused by the demonic numerous times.

9

GOD THE DECIDER

When the church loses sight of God's purpose to establish his kingdom on earth with us as his fellow heirs, distortions of the gospel inevitably follow. We will consider a few of these. First our going to heaven when we die becomes our sole hope for life after death. Our hope is reduced to glorifying God by joining in heaven's never-ending praise. Evangelists often ask, "Where will you spend eternity? Will you spend it in heaven or hell?" Their gospel is never-ending life in either the glory of heaven or the torment of hell. The word *spend* leaves the impression that time continues throughout eternity. Embedded in this is a misunderstanding of eternal. Both in the Greek and the Hebrew, the words that describe hell mean a long time or without a fixed end. They do not mean everlasting or never-ending.

The truth is that only God is eternal. To be eternal is to be without beginning or ending. All else, including hell and time, is created reality. With the coming of the kingdom, time itself will be no more. Heaven, hell, and earth will all pass away when they are transformed by the coming of the kingdom. Then God will be "all in all" (Romans 15: 28), and all will be eternal. I view threatening persons with never-ending torment in hell as spiritual abuse. This calls into question the goodness and justice of God. Imagining God forever tormenting someone makes trusting him more difficult, not less. By proclaiming hell as never-ending, "we are found to be misrepresenting God" (Romans 15: 15).

Here are a few better questions to ask: What is eternal life? How might we best describe it? From our side, it is life lived before God. Eternal life is not dependent upon our being aware that our lives are being lived in God's presence. Nevertheless, our every moment is lived before him. Our lives are lived in relationship with him. There will be many moments when we will be aware of God's presence and even more when we won't. Still his eye is on the sparrow, and we can know he always watches us! "And this is eternal life, that they may know you, the only true God, and Jesus Christ whom you have sent" (John 17:3). There's a *knowing that he knows us* in eternal life. When we respond in faith to the gospel, we receive eternal life and live our lives in response to the call of Christ.

Looking at it from God's side, it is his face turned toward us. The light of God's countenance is upon us. God chooses to be in relationship with us. He commits himself to us and remains faithful to his decision to be for us. He lives in us, and we live in him. He places us in right relationship with him. He calls us to follow Jesus and leads us day by day.

This lets us see another destructive flaw in the way many evangelists present the gospel. Often eternal life is made to be entirely dependent on what we decide. If we decide to accept Jesus, we will have eternal life. If not, we won't. Our decision determines our ultimate future. If this is the case, then our decision matters more than God's. God is left with nothing to do but yield to our decision. This makes us more powerful than God. Or at the very least, this places our decisions on the same level as God's. This makes us God's equal. In effect, we become our own God.

To illustrate, I was opposed to going to war with Iraq. But that was not my decision. It was the president who determined what we would do. My decision was not on the same plane with his. I didn't have the power to decide this. He did. We were not equals in terms of power. It was not possible for my decision to mean as much as his. Neither is it possible for our decisions to mean as much as God's. President Bush famously said, "I am the decider!" Our God is the decider, and he has already decided to be for us! "For God has imprisoned all in disobedience so that he may be merciful to all" (Romans 12:32).

When eternal life is defined as we've described, then it is unaffected by location. We don't have to die and go to heaven to enter eternal life. Eternal life begins here and continues in heaven. When we receive eternal life, we enter the kingdom of God. So there's a sense in which eternal life is not fully complete until God's entire creation shares in the coming kingdom. This recognizes that we don't exist as isolated individuals. We live in relationship to God, others, and the creation. When at last death is swallowed up in victory for the whole creation, then eternal life will have come to completion. And we will be at home in the new creation. This helps us recognize that God has a future. It is to "make his home among mortals" (Revelation 21:3) and to receive from all creation the glory and praise that he is due!

When God is the ultimate decider, we're able to see that he is able to relate to us apart from our decisions. This opens the way for God to extend eternal life to children and even the unborn. God is not bound by their lack of a decision to accept Jesus. This is so for adults as well.

His hands are not tied by our rejection of him. St. Paul's conversion demonstrates that God is not required to relate to us as we relate to him. Saul was actively persecuting Christians—and along with them Jesus— when Jesus appeared to him on the road to Damascus (Acts 9:1–9). In spite of his rejection and persecution, God chose Paul "to bring my name before Gentiles and kings and before the people of Israel" (Acts 9:15).

Paul wrestles with this issue for his own people in chapters 9, 10, and 11 of the book of Romans. He begins chapter 9 with his "great sorrow and unceasing agony" over the failure of his people to accept Christ. He begins chapter 11 by asking if this means that God has rejected his people. He answers, "By no means!" He points to his own conversion as proving this. He compares his people to branches of an olive tree that were broken off so that the Gentiles could be grafted on. But they still may be grafted back in, "for God has the power to graft them in again" (Romans 11:23).

He brings his argument to a conclusion in verse 32, which reads, "For God has imprisoned all in disobedience so that he may be merciful to all." In this way God retains his freedom to extend eternal life to anyone. Paul and John both speak of persons as lost in this present age but never in the age to come. Since God is inexhaustible, unconditional, forgiving love, we may hope that his mercy will ultimately extend to all. But since our interpretations of Scripture are not infallible, we cannot say with certainty this will or will not be the case. Those who claim otherwise know too much.

The bottom line is that God always remains free to act as he chooses. He wouldn't be God were that not true. He also remains committed to his Word, his purposes, his people, and his promises. He wouldn't be righteous if this was not true. Because he desires to be in an intimate and loving relationship with us, we can experience eternal life now by repenting and believing the gospel. Faith can create an experience of salvation, but salvation itself was created by God acting in Christ, not by us.

In their efforts to get persons saved, I've sometimes heard preachers exhorting people to come to Christ "before it is everlastingly too late!" The assumption is that if we die before we accept Christ there is nothing more God can do. This makes death more powerful than God. Death shuts the door on God's opportunity to extend eternal life to anyone. Death ties God's hands forever. This amounts to a denial of Christ overcoming death. This ignores the numerous times in the Bible that Jesus and God's people raise the dead. The good news is, through Christ, the power of death over us has been broken! Romans 14:8–9 reads, "If we live, we live to the Lord, and if we die, we die to the Lord; so then, whether we live or whether we die, we are the Lord's. For to this end Christ died and lived again, so that he might be Lord of both the dead and the living." God has made Jesus Lord of all. Death cannot altar this.

An older version of the Apostles' Creed declared, "He descended into hell." First Peter 4:6 announces his purpose in doing so. "For this is the reason the gospel was proclaimed even to the dead, so that, though they had been judged in the flesh as everyone is judged, they might live in the spirit as God does." Here eternal life is offered to the already judged dead.

Evangelists often insist on the need to be biblical while they ignore the beliefs and practices of the New Testament church. First Corinthians 15:29 shows that at least some in the church believed God to be able to save the already dead. This Scripture reads, "Otherwise, what will those people do who receive baptism on behalf of the dead? If the dead are not raised at all, *why are people baptized on their behalf?*" Paul does not indicate whether he supports this practice or not. But his asking this question shows us that this was happening in the early church.

In a situation where extreme immorality was defiling the church, Paul instructs the church to "hand this man over to Satan for the destruction of the flesh, so that his spirit may be saved in the day of the Lord" (1 Corinthians 5:5). Death, Satan, and all the powers of hell are not to be compared to the love of God that frees us from the prison of death. The gospel is that Jesus is the Lord, not death!

Colossians 1:19–20 declares, "For in him all the fullness of God was pleased to dwell, and through him God was pleased to reconcile to himself all things, whether on earth or in heaven, by making peace through the blood of the cross." Thus, Christ died for all the living. His cross opens the way for eternal life to be extended to the creation itself. Christ's death and resurrection was for us and all creation. With his resurrection, the creation, too, is put on the way toward transformation. Thus, God is not only preparing a place for us in heaven. He is also preparing a place for us in the coming new creation. When we fail to see this, we are left with heaven as the only world for our living in eternal life when we die.

The Methodist funeral service begins with John 11:25–26, which reads, "Jesus said, I am the resurrection and the life, he who believes in me, though he die, yet shall he live, and whosoever lives and believes in me shall never die." With this statement, Jesus affirms his holding the present and future lives of believers in his strong hands. Anyone who believes in him dies but yet lives. John 5:24 reads, "Very truly I tell you, whoever believes has eternal life, and does not come under judgment, but has passed from death to life." John 6:47 reads, "Very Truly I tell you, whoever believes has eternal life."

While death belongs to this world, death is excluded from the kingdom and eternal life. For the Bible, death is an enemy and not a friend. It's the last enemy to be destroyed (1 Corinthians 15:26). The conquest of death for believers will be experienced by them at their deaths. All creation will experience this when God makes all things new.

10

WHAT ABOUT HELL?

The wrath of God is another huge slice of the missing gospel in many mainline Protestant denominations. This and preaching "hellfire and damnation" has nearly become extinct. Jesus said, "Do not fear those who kill the body but cannot kill the soul; rather fear him who can destroy both soul and body in hell" (Matthew 10:28). In this and in numerous other texts the Bible calls us to fear both God and hell. But for the most part this has been missing gospel in my own ministry. I view this as a serious omission in my preaching and teaching.

The wrath of God and hell are both well attested to in Scripture. If God is free to act as he chooses, then he is as free to give us over to wrath and hell as he is to lead us into eternal life. If he faithfully keeps his promises, wrath and hell must be as real as heaven since all three are present in Scripture. The failure to include these in the churches preaching and teaching contributes to persons imagining God to be a benevolent being that is indifferent to human sin. We've often been told that God is unconditional love. So many have concluded that God's relating to us is unaffected by our decisions and behaviors. If that was really true, our decisions to believe or to seek his will or do our own would have no effect on our relationship with him. But the truth is that God does take these things seriously. They do affect how he relates to us. There are blessing to be realized by trusting and obeying him, and there is a terrible cost in rejecting and disobeying him. We've considered many of the blessings that come to those who trust and obey. Now we'll consider some of the cost when we fail to do so.

We'll begin by asking, "What is God's wrath? How does God express his wrath?" God's wrath is his anger directed toward sin, evil, and us when we cooperate with our own enslavement. God's wrath is expressed by his handing us over to our own way. He lets us have what we have chosen. He gives us over to the consequences of those choices.

After he considers some of the behaviors of humankind, Paul writes, "Therefore, *God gave them up* in the lusts of their hearts to impurity, to the degrading of their bodies among themselves" (Romans 1:24). The twenty-sixth verse reads, "For this reason *God gave them up* to degrading passions." The twenty-eighth verse reads, "And since they did not see fit to acknowledge God, *God gave them up* to a debased mind and to things that should not be done." *God's wrath is expressed by his letting us go!*

We are not necessary for God's well-being. It was out of love and not necessity that he created humankind. He is not like a codependent parent who is so enmeshed in his children that he can't bear to see them suffer. Neither is he so weak and needy that he can't endure whatever grief he feels when we choose to go our own way without him. Neither is he indifferent to our behavior, not caring enough to react to us at all. A god who remained indifferent to sin and evil would himself be evil!

One Sabbath day Jesus entered a synagogue where a man with a withered hand was present. The Pharisees looked on, hoping to find a way to accuse him. After he called the man to him, Jesus asked them if it was lawful to do good or to do harm, to save life or to kill on the Sabbath? But they were silent. Then "Jesus looked around at them with anger; he was grieved at their hardness of heart" (Mark 3: 5). Paul admonishes us to be careful how we live so as "to not grieve the Holy Spirit of God" (Ephesians 4:30). God experiences both anger and grief.

Because Christ is always with those who've received eternal life, we may grieve God and provoke him to anger, but nothing in all creation will be able to separate us from his love. But Scripture teaches this is not the case with those God has given up. The wrath of God rests on them. John 3:36 reads, "He who believes in the son has eternal life; he who does not believe in the son shall not see life, but the wrath of God rests upon him." Those who do not believe "perish" (John 3: 16). Paul asks if God is unjust to inflict wrath upon us. He answers his question with a question. "By no means! How else could God judge the world?" (Romans 3: 6).

Scripture describes the last judgment in Matthew 25:31– 46. All the nations appear before Christ, who separates them as a shepherd separates sheep from goats. They are separated based on what they did and did not do for the least of these. Neither the sheep nor the goats recognized Jesus to be present when they responded to the needs before them. The goats are sent away to eternal punishment while the righteous enter eternal life.

The last judgment in Revelation 20:11–15 paints a similar picture. The books are opened, and the dead are judged according to their recorded works. "Anyone whose name was not found written in the book of life was thrown into the lake of fire." Revelation 20:7 reads, "And the devil who deceived them was thrown into the lake of fire and sulfur, where the beast and the false prophet were, and they were tormented forever and ever." From these and numerous other Scriptures, hell has been understood to be a place of never-ending torment. All those God's wrath rests on go to hell when they die.

Revelation 21 begins with John seeing a new heaven and a new earth and the Holy City coming down out of heaven. He hears a loud voice announcing God's dwelling among mortals, wiping away their tears, and saying that there will be no more death. He hears God say that "he is making all things new." Then in verse 8 God says: "But as for the cowardly, the faithless, the polluted, the murders, the fornicators, the sorcerers, the idolaters and all liars, their place will be in the lake that burns with fire and sulfur, which is the second death." After describing the Holy City, verse 27 reads, "But nothing unclean will enter it not anyone who practices abomination or falsehood, but only those who are written in the book of life." Here in the very chapter that provides us with the most detailed picture of God's ultimate salvation, these verses declare the destiny of some to be the lake of fire.

The verses we have considered and many we have not allow us to hope that in the end "that at the name of Jesus every knee should bend, in heaven and on earth and under the earth, and every tongue should confess that Jesus Christ is Lord, to the glory of God the Father" (Philippians 2:10–11). While universal salvation is clearly not certain, the possibility that all will be saved is present in Scripture—enough so that we cannot close the door into the final kingdom on anyone.

Even so, most of the New Testament declares hell to be the final home of the faithless. Both the Old Testament and the New reveal God to be fully capable of destroying both individuals and nations. Jesus saw hell to be both real and terrible. Mark 1:42–48 reads,

> If any of you put a stumbling block before one of these little ones who believe in me, it would be better for you if a great millstone were hung around your neck and you were thrown into the sea. If your hand causes you to stumble, cut it off; it is better for you to enter life maimed than to have two hands and to go to hell, to the unquenchable fire. And if your foot causes you to stumble cut it off; it is better for you to enter life lame than to have two feet and to be thrown into hell. And if your eye causes you to stumble, tear it out; it is better for you to enter the kingdom of God with one eye than to have two eyes and to be thrown into hell, where the worm never dies, and the fire is never quenched.

It would be hard to imagine a stronger warming and a clearer teaching of the terribleness of hell than this. The fire described as "never quenched" seems to point to a never-ending hell.

An examination of church traditions confirms that for the great majority of denominations throughout church history, hell has been understood to be the ultimate destiny of those who fail to accept God's offer of salvation through faith in Christ. Hell has usually but not always been understood to be never-ending. Anyone who has experienced excruciating pain knows that minutes can seem like hours. The horrific pains of hell may seem to be never-ending to those in hell. Psalm 30:5 declares, "For his anger is but for a moment; his favor is for a lifetime. Weeping may linger for the night but joy comes with the morning." Since God limits his anger in this life, why wouldn't he in hell? A never-ending hell would leave God unable to make "all things new."

Since there is no mention of hell being present after God makes all things new, I'm unable to imagine how hell could possibly be never-ending. This plus hell being a created reality and not eternal in itself is enough to convince me that this can't possibly be the case. Therefore, I think of hell as belonging to this age but not to the age to come. As long as this world continues so will hell. But this world is passing away! And when it does, so will hell! This is good news for anyone who fears a loved one has gone to a never-ending hell.

Scripture and church tradition teach that hell is real. But what if hell is sustained to prepare us to share his coming kingdom on earth? If so, the question is this: How might this possibly be the case? Hebrews 12:1–12 gives us a way to understand how this might be true. The writer exhorts the church "not to regard lightly the discipline of the Lord when you are punished by him; for the Lord disciplines those whom he loves, and chastises every child whom he accepts." He reminds them that their human parents disciplined them and they respected them, so they should be even more willing to be disciplined by the Lord, who does so in order that they might share his holiness. Thus, God's punishment serves his purpose to reshape us into his likeness.

If this is so here and now, why wouldn't this also be true in hell? If so, punishment in hell is not for the purpose of pouring out God's rage for man's sinfulness. In his death on the cross Jesus has suffered all of that for us. God is love. I believe God's power sustains hell for love's purposes. Love's great purpose is to prepare us for the kingdom. I believe God is at work in hell for that purpose with those who respond to him. We know that God is at work for good in all things for those who love the Lord. He's also at work for good in all things for all those he loves. Although he hates sin, he loves the sinner. Because God is good, hell's suffering serves his good purposes. Hell does not change God. It changes people!

This can be seen in the story of the rich man and Lazarus found in Luke 16:19–31. The rich man who's in agony in hell calls out to Abraham and Lazarus in heaven and begs Abraham to send someone to warn his brothers so that they will repent. In hell he has seen the value of repentance for himself and his brothers. We know that suffering is a great teacher. We spank our children or send them to time-out or deprive them of some treat in order to teach them that certain behaviors are unacceptable. Lessons learned through suffering are not easily forgotten.

Love knows that suffering can be valuable. After he celebrates the hope of sharing the glory of God, Paul writes in Romans 5:3–5, "And not only that, but we boast in our suffering knowing that suffering produces endurance, and endurance produces character, and character produces hope, and hope does not disappoint us, because God's love has been poured into our hearts through the Holy Spirit that has been given to us." If God uses suffering to produce good in this life, why not in hell?

Psalms 139:7–8 declares; "Where can I go from your spirit? Or where can I flee from your presence? If I ascend to heaven, you are there; if make my bed in Sheol (hell) you are there." God in the person of the Holy Spirit is present even in hell. The psalmist realized this prior to Christ's descent into hell, which is revealed in the New Testament. What is new with the arrival of Christ in hell is the gates of hell have been thrown open. They can no longer prevail over anyone. Matthew 16:18 assures the church that "the gates of hell will not prevail against it." Since this is true for the church in the power of the Holy Spirit, it most assuredly is true for the Holy Spirit present in hell.

When we recognize this, our question becomes this: "What does the Holy Spirit achieve in hell?" Mark 9:45 reads; "For everyone will be salted with fire." This is a correcting fire that applies to both the living and the dead. As surely as God disciplines us here, he disciplines those in hell. God's correcting fire works to consume the sin that leaves his children blind. The Holy Spirit works to bring us to the truth. Through his suffering, the rich man realized that repentance could save his brothers from hell. Having enabled him to see this for his brothers, why not for himself as well? Jesus invited those who are weak and heavy-laden to come to him and receive rest (Matthew 11:28). It may be that the Spirit also offers the same to those in hell who've been made ready to respond. The rich man's experience in hell created a new desire. While he lived, his priority was the enjoyment of his riches. Now he desperately wants his brothers to repent. His new desire is evidence of his own repentance. He has a new openness to the Holy Spirit. The Spirit working through the sufferings of hell is responsible for this. Why would the Holy Spirit use hell to create this change if escaping hell was impossible?

Jesus told the disciples, "It is easier for a camel to go through the eye of a needle than for someone who is rich to enter the kingdom of God." When the disciples heard this, they were greatly astounded and said, "Then who can be saved?" But Jesus looked at them and said, "For mortals it is impossible, but for God all things are possible" (Matthew

19:23–26). Jesus makes it clear that salvation is in God's hands, not ours. Since this is so, we can't make escaping hell impossible.

Revelation 3:19–22 reads,

> I reprove and discipline those whom I love. Be earnest, therefore, and repent. Listen! I am standing at the door knocking; if you hear my voice and open the door, I will come in to you and eat with you, and you with me. To the one who conquers I will give a place with me on my throne, just as I myself conquered and sat down with my Father on his throne. Let anyone who has an ear listen to what the Spirit is saying to the churches.

This message was delivered to the church at Laodicea. But it's also addressed to "anyone who has an ear." The rich man is pictured as speaking with and hearing Abraham. Then surely he has an ear to hear the call of the Holy Spirit.

Much of what I've written about the rich man in hell is speculative imagination on my part. I've written as I have to encourage us to ask good questions. Since in Christ all things are possible, we may "hope all things" (1 Corinthians 13:7). We are admonished in Scripture to be ready to account for the hope that is within us. So the question is this: "Why are we entitled to have any hope for those in hell? What is the basis for our hope for them?"

To adequately answer we must first ask, "What took place when Jesus ascended into heaven?" Usually the focus of the gospel is on the meaning of the cross and resurrection for us. The meaning of the ascension is rarely emphasized. But this aspect of the gospel is crucial for us and our Lord. The church's failure to understand and present this element of the gospel has left millions without the hope that the ascension provides.

So what is the critical meaning of the ascension? What new hope does the ascension offer? This is when Jesus became Lord of all! Jesus was enthroned as Lord when he ascended into heaven. Then and there God made him Lord of heaven and earth! Now he "has the keys to Death and Hades" (Revelation 1:18). He holds both in his strong, nail-pierced hands. "Jesus is Lord," is the cornerstone of the gospel in the New Testament. This is the good news our hope ultimately rests on. Acts 2:36 reads, "Therefore let the entire house of Israel know with certainty that God has made him both Lord and Messiah, this Jesus whom you crucified."

First Peter tells us that prior to his ascension Jesus descended into hell and proclaimed the gospel even to the dead so that they might "live in the spirit as God does." This Scripture makes it clear that death does not mean it is "everlastingly too late" for anyone in hell. In this life we believe our faith response to the gospel brings eternal life. According to 1 Peter, this is true for those in hell as well.

It is the crucified Christ that God has made Lord of all. It was his only Son who suffered and died for the sins of the world and who descended into hell and ascended into heaven. It's Jesus who on the cross prayed, "Father, forgive them; for they know not what they are doing" (Luke 23:34), that reigns in hell. This prayer expresses God's will for his enemies. It is Christ who cried, "My god, My God, why have you forsaken me?" (Matthew 27:46). It is Christ who is present with those given over to hell. At the cross he took upon himself God's wrath that they earned through their arrogant disobedience. According to Ephesians 4:8, "When he ascended on high he made captivity it's self a captive." This verse declares that hell itself has been captured by Christ. Christ has made hell his prisoner. Since this is so, all those imprisoned in hell are in his hands. Now that the crucified Christ reigns in hell, we can keep hope alive. We're not compelled to give up hope for anyone who may have entered hell. I believe Christ is present in hell to bring life to all who respond to him. I believe all those in hell who receive life in the Holy Spirit are relieved of their suffering. Christ takes their suffering upon himself and overcomes it. That's what God's sacrificial love does at the cross and in the deepest hell. It may be that they are ultimately escorted by an angel to one of heaven's rooms.

Why else would God have enthroned Christ as Lord in hell? If hell's primary purpose is punishment, why is the Holy Spirit present to proclaim the gospel? Throughout Israel's long history God proved himself fully capable of both punishing people and putting people to death. He does not need the Holy Spirit's presence in hell to manage this. His leaving them in hell is all that's needed. I believe the Holy Spirit is there for the same reason he is present here—to enable persons to repent, to save people from destruction and prepare them for their unique place in the kingdom of God.

Some of those in hell may be among the people that make up the nations that will have a place in the coming kingdom (Revelation 21:24–26). John saw the nations as the pagan peoples who were seduced by the great whore and trampled the Holy City (Jerusalem) underfoot. They were finally overcome by the armies of heaven (Revelation 11:2, 18:3, and 19:15). If these heathen enemies of God are present in the final kingdom as "the nations," then anyone might be. Here God accepts entire nations in spite of their persecutions, not just a single individual as in Paul's case. They are unbelievers, whereas Paul was a zealous believer in God. If God is going to include at least some unbelieving nations in his coming kingdom, who can we exclude?

I'm not saying that everyone in hell will ultimately trust our crucified Lord. This is not for us to know. I believe our Lord continues to respect the choices we make. It may be that some will fail to respond to him. It may be that their future is to ultimately perish. However, the crucified Christ is still the judge. He is the decider. We cannot make our decisions as meaningful as his. If this were so, there would be no hope for the enemies of God. To make our decisions as meaningful as his is to make us God's equal. We become as God, and God is reduced to being human.

72

I believe our ultimate end is the kingdom of God on earth. As for those in hell, who will or will not be a part of the final kingdom is not ours to know. Our not knowing is good news for all those who've suffered unspeakable grief in believing that those in hell suffer endless torment. Those who proclaim this make themselves infallible interpreters of Scripture and suggest they are as all-knowing as God. Our claiming to know the ultimate future of anyone or any group in hell amounts to our playing God. There's a strong tendency throughout church history to know too much. These beliefs include suggesting that outside a particular church there is no salvation and that the destiny of all nonbelievers is eternal torment in hell. These beliefs have brought great suffering on countless believers. I hope what I have written will relieve their suffering, not add to it.

11

THE CROSS, THE ANCHOR THAT SECURES HOPE

I dare not anchor my hope solely in my spiritual e xperiences or my interpretations of Scripture. I could be deceived or deceiving myself. We humans seem to have an endless capacity for self-deception. But "if God is for us, who is against us?" (Romans 8: 31). In his free grace God decided to create humankind for himself and for us. Scripture declares he decided this "before the foundation of the world." Our hope is ultimately grounded in God's decision for us, not in our decision for him. The decisive evidence for his decision is the cross. The cross of Christ provides a firm foundation for our hope.

Psychologically we know we tend to see what we are looking for. I believe much of the suffering caused by flawed beliefs is rooted in this tendency. It's often been said that the Bible can be made to prove almost anything. Beliefs depend on the Scriptures chosen and how they are applied. Numerous Scriptures describe hell as endless torment.

Others anticipate hell as being emptied through the power of the Holy Spirit. Some Scriptures expect the destruction of the world. Others expect its transformation. Most look forward to the reality of heaven, but some anticipate that the dead sleep until the resurrection on the last day. Since Scriptures can be found to support opposing views, we can't employ Scripture to settle every critical issue, especially those related to hell. Those who are drawn to emphasize the unending horrors of hell dismiss the verses that dispute this view. The reverse is true as well. So the question is this: Is there a way to escape this trap? If so, what do we need to do?

Yes, there is, but only one way. To do so we must turn our eyes upon the cross of Christ. When our eyes are on the most threatening passages in the Bible, we lose sight of the cross and the victory that our Lord won there. When Martin Luther was struggling with his fear of being predestined for rejection, his spiritual adviser counseled him to look upon the wounds of Christ. He assured him that in light of Christ's wounds, the question of predestination would "cease of itself," and it did. When he focused on the cross, his fear of rejection and hell gave way to faith and hope.

Our creative imagination can serve us well too. If we ask the Holy Spirit to help us imagine ourselves at the foot of the cross, with our eyes on our Savior's suffering for us, then hope without limits can be ours. The church has always understood the cross to be an atonement for our sins. Through the sacrificial death of Christ, God reconciled the world to himself (2 Corinthians 5:19). Some churches interpret this to be true for all mankind, others only for those who are predestined to be redeemed. Scripture proclaims, "God so loved the world." Here the world should be taken literally. The many references to the whole creation participating in the coming kingdom make this clear.

Seven major theories of the atonement have been proposed as the way to understand the death of Jesus. The penal substitution theory, which was formulated by the sixteenth-century reformers, is the one usually preached in Catholic and Protestant churches and by evangelists. Briefly this theory states that Christ bore the punishment for sin in our place. The righteousness of the law and the holiness of God are satisfied by his substitutional death for us. If this is your understanding of the meaning of the cross, then look upon his wounds and know that Christ paid the penalty for our sins. Justice has been served. God is satisfied. You have been set free.

There is still more good news to be seen at the cross. Both God the Father and Jesus the Son suffer there. God experiences the suffering and death of his only Son for our sake. The innocent suffer for the guilty. The cross reveals that there are no limits in God's love. My unlimited hope is drawn from God's unlimited, suffering love, which was displayed in Jesus' cross. We have the capacity to empathize with others and to vicariously experience what another person is feeling. In a limited way we can put ourselves in another person's place. In effect, we take someone else into ourselves.

When I turn my eyes on the cross, I see something comparable yet infinitely more profound happening there. In his unlimited empathy, I see Christ taking into himself sin, death, and evil. All three of these are powers that capture us, powers that God alone can overcome. In his suffering and death I see Christ drawing these powers into himself.

With his resurrection, I see God our Father breaking their power over us and all creation. Thus, Paul writes, "For our sake he made him to be sin who knew no sin, so that in him we might become the righteousness of God" (2 Corinthians 5: 21).

This view is akin to the Christus Victor understanding of the atonement. This name was taken from a groundbreaking book by Gustaf Aulen, a book first published in 1931. His understanding was drawn from the ransom theory that was predominant in the early church for the first thousand years of church history. Aulen wrote, "The work of Christ is first and foremost a victory over the powers that hold mankind in bondage: sin, death, and the devil." I fully agree with this, but I would want to make a significant addition to his statement. I would add the words *and creation* after the word mankind. The creation itself is also in bondage to death and decay and "waits with eager longing for the revealing of the children of God" (Romans 8:19). Then "the creation itself will be set free from its bondage to decay and will obtain the freedom of the glory of the children of God" (Romans 8: 21).

The breaking of the power of death over creation has not been included in any previous theory of the atonement. Here is another critical element of the gospel that has been missing. *It is crucial because it confirms God's intention to free the creation for transformation, not destruction.* The cross of Christ would be emptied of its meaning for creation if this world was completely destroyed when all things are made new. The creation would have waited in vain. Paul's hope for this creation would be a false hope. All Scriptures that look forward to this world becoming the kind of place where the wolf and the lamb will lay down together would be in error.

The inclusion of the creation in Christ's victory over death means salvation for this world, not destruction and death. So Paul writes, "We know that the whole creation has been groaning in labor pains until now; and not only the creation, but we ourselves, who have the first fruits of the Spirit, groan inwardly while we wait for adoption, the redemption of our bodies" (Romans 8:22–23). Paul's vision for this world is similar to his vision for himself. Like himself, the world groans as it waits for adoption. He groans as he waits for the redemption of the body, not just the soul. And he waits with the world for its transformation, not its destruction. Paul expects the redemption of us and the world, not our escape from the world.

Genesis 2:7 reads, "Then the Lord God formed man from the dust of the ground and breathed into his nostrils the breath of life, and the man became a living being." God created man from the previously created world. Human life was created from nature. In our bodily existence we live intimately connected with and dependent on nature. Like man's creation in the beginning, the new creation will be formed from this world. The new creation will bring a redemption of nature. Since we are so joined with nature, a new creation would seem to be necessary if we are to reign in our resurrected bodies on earth. Because the whole person, including our bodies, is to participate in the kingdom, Paul waits for the new creation.

The world's recreation establishes a world without sin, death, evil, disease, violence, greed, and all other sources of suffering. It is to be a world suitable to host and participate in the eternal kingdom of God. It will provide the context for the healing of all those included in the nations. It will be a world where justice is established for all, including God. God will then receive the praise and glory that is due him from all creation.

The Bible makes it clear that Jesus appeared to his disciples in a resurrected body—a new transformed body that bore the scars of his earthly body. His body is a new creation. The one and only resurrected body to date! He ascended into heaven in his resurrected body. First Corinthians 15:20–23 reads, "But in fact Christ has been raised from the dead, the first fruits of those who have died. For since death came through a human being, the resurrection of the dead has also come through a human being; for as all die in Adam, *so all will be made alive in Christ*. But each in his own order: Christ the first fruits, then at his coming those who belong to Christ." When Christ returns, we will receive resurrected bodies like his. We will then be fully one with him in heart, mind, and body. When this is achieved, we will be enthroned beside him in the completed kingdom of God. Enthronement with Christ is the future the Bible promises to "those who conquer" (Revelation 21:7). It is not realized by just being born. It is promised to those who believe and take up their cross and follow Jesus. It is promised to those who suffer with him.

There is another experience that should be noted but is rarely mentioned in our churches. In spite of our regularly praying the Lord's Prayer in our worship services, we've lost sight of this. When we pray "lead us not into temptation but deliver us from evil," how many of us understand what we are praying for? Some assume we are asking God not to tempt us. But James 1:13 reads, "No one, when tempted, should say, I am being tempted by God; for God cannot be tempted by evil and he himself tempts no one." James addresses our being tested in a number of verses. This shows that this had become an issue in the early church as well. The difference is that they were aware of this while we usually are not.

So what are we asking when we pray this clause of the Lord's Prayer? In the garden of Gethsemane Jesus told the disciples "to pray that you may not come into the time of trail" (Mark 14:38). "Lead us not into temptation" is asking that our faith not be put on trail. We are also asking that God preserve us when we are tested. When we pray for God to "deliver us from evil," we are asking him to bring us through the test. The following words of Jesus have been preserved in church tradition, although they are not found in the Bible: "No one can obtain the kingdom of heaven who has not passed through testing." Although this would not be true of young children, this expresses the expectation that followers of Jesus will be tested. The presence of this clause in the Lord's Prayer shows Jesus expected this to be the case. When we pray to be delivered from evil, we are asking God to keep us from falling away in times of trail or testing. Some denominations teach that falling away is impossible. The presence of this clause in the Lord's Prayer demonstrates that Jesus believed it was possible to fall into the hands of the Devil.

The expectation that we will be tested brings us to one of the most important and controversial issues for the followers of Jesus. On the one hand, numerous Scriptures assure us of eternal security. But the Lord's Prayer and numerous other Scriptures assume the possibility of falling away. Hebrews 6:4–6 reads,

> For it is impossible to restore again to repentance those who have once been enlightened, and have tasted the heavenly gift, and have shared the Holy Spirit, and have tasted the goodness of the word of God and the powers of the age to come, and then fallen away, since on their own they are crucifying again the son of God and are holding him up to contempt.

Here even those whose experience of Christ is especially powerful are at risk of losing their salvation. Some denominations teach "once saved always saved." While others like my own teach that it is possible to lose our faith and be lost. Since much scriptural evidence can be advanced for both positions, we can't resolve this issue by simply quoting Scripture. Here again we need to look to the cross of Christ.

On the cross Christ took upon himself our rejection. He suffered our condemnation there. In his abandonment by his Father, he suffered the agonies of those who fall into the hands of the Devil. There he suffered our damnation and true and total hell. In doing so, he crushed their power. He put death and hell to death. In his descent into hell he gathered to himself those suffering there. When we see these things happening through his suffering and death, we realize that the cross amounts to more than satisfying God's justice and holiness. We see that even if we fall into the hands of the Devil, Christ is with us. We see that because he is with us, the Devil and hell cannot hold us. When we see these things, we recognize that our loss of faith is not to be compared to God's decision to bring us into the kingdom. His decision to allow his Son to suffer at the hands of the Devil so that we might escape both the Devil and hell decides the issue.

So at the very least there is no necessity that those who fall away will ultimately be lost. The events of the cross, resurrection, and ascension have established Jesus Christ as Lord. The last judgment has been given to him. He will return "to judge the quick and the dead." Because it is the crucified Lord who will be our judge, we are assured that we have nothing to fear from him. Whether all or only a few are saved, our crucified Lord will be the judge and decider. Believing these things to be true, it's hard for me to imagine anyone who has fallen away being left out of the coming kingdom. Falling away is not the unforgivable sin. Jesus, who suffered and died so that all might be forgiven, will forgive all who are willing to be forgiven.

But we must take seriously Scriptures like this one in Hebrews that warn against our falling away. Therefore, we need to ask if it is possible that both sides of the eternal security question might be right. I see a way that this might prove to be the case. If when we are tested, it is our being seated on Christ's throne to rule with him that is at stake, not sharing in the kingdom itself. If this is so, it may be that those who fall away will be included in the nations that Revelation declares will be present in the coming kingdom. Since those who make up the nations are the disbelieving enemies of God that persecuted his people, why not include believers who've fallen away as well? This is speculation on my part. The Bible does not reveal what persons or nations will make up the nations. But even if this should be the outcome and we were to gain the whole world when we fall away, this would not compare with what we would have lost! Whatever the case, enthronement with Christ in the kingdom to come is so unimaginably great that our paying any price or enduring any suffering is not to be compared with this! So forgetting what lies behind, let's press on to this high calling in Christ Jesus.

Hebrews speaking of our "crucifying again the Lord" reminds us that both our actions and inactions can wound our Lord. As long as this world exists, our Lord will suffer with and from human sinfulness. Thus far we've considered many of the benefits that will be ours and the creations with the arrival of the kingdom. We've also said that God will receive the praise and glory he is due. His exposure to pain by our actions will also end. I've often heard people say, "The world has become so wicked I don't see how God can put up with it much longer." Words to this effect express our intuitive sense that God does indeed suffer along with his world. His suffering will end on the last day. He will realize His purpose for creating, sustaining, redeeming, and suffering for and with the world when we become joint heirs with him of all things. Joy for the world will mean joy for God as well.

The cross reveals God to be passionate, suffering, unlimited love. Those who've been filled to overflowing with this love know that he loves others, not just themselves. They know he loves the world that he created. The creation of the world and the resurrection of Jesus reveal God's unlimited power. The only limitations to his power are those he has imposed on himself. Since God is both unlimited love and unlimited power, we can be sure he will bring about all that he has promised. This book offers some answers to the question, "What can we hope for?" Faith trusts the decision God has made for our salvation. Hope lives with eyes on God's promises. Hope anticipates God's enabling us to suffer what we must suffer and to do what he calls us to do.

The hope of heaven is the final hope of the great majority of Christians. But hope in the New Testament does not end in heaven. Thus, Paul wrote, "But our citizenship is in heaven, and it is from there we are expecting a savior, the Lord Jesus Christ. He will transform the body of our humiliation that it may be conformed to the body of his glory" (Philippians 3:20–21). Yet hope for the resurrection of our bodies and God's kingdom on earth has faded into the background. But both hope of heaven and hope for the kingdom and our place within it are legitimate New Testament hopes! Holding these authentic hopes keeps us on the path toward sharing Jesus' throne!

12

Jesus the Presenter

Hebrews 12: 2 reads, "Looking to Jesus, the pioneer and perfecter of our faith, who for the sake of the joy set before him endured the cross." God the Father and Jesus the Son envisioned the completion of salvation's story. The joy before them in their shared vision enabled Jesus to suffer the cross and God to suffer the death of his only Son. The divine vision is filled with unspeakable joy. The joy they envision is Christ reconciling the world to God and his no longer counting our trespasses against us. The joy they envision is the salvation of God's creation. The joy they envision is our becoming kings and priests with Christ, bringing healing to the nations in the coming kingdom. Anticipating this for humankind means joy for the Father and the Son.

Jesus anticipated the joy that would be his when he brought us into the kingdom of heaven. Jesus suffered the cross, anticipating the joy that would be his when the salvation and transformation of all creation is complete. *Jesus anticipated the joy that would be his when he hands over the entire redeemed creation to his Father! Jesus anticipated the joy all creation will share when he hands over the kingdom to God and God becomes "all in all."* Jesus anticipated the joy that will be ours when we share his throne. Jesus anticipated the oneness in love and joy that we will share with him and his Father forever. The Holy Spirit flooded him with joy as he anticipated the redemption he would bring to God's world.

First Corinthians 15:22–28 describes the final event in salvation's story. It reads, "For as all die in Adam, so all will be made alive in Christ. But each in his own order; Christ the first fruits, than at his coming those who belong to Christ. Then comes the end, when he hands over the kingdom to God the Father, after he has destroyed every ruler and every authority and power. For he must reign until he has put all his enemies under his feet. The last enemy to be destroyed is death. For the Father has put all things in subjection under the Sons feet. But when it says, "All things are put in subjection," it is obvious that this

> does not include the Father, who put all things in subjection under the *Son*. When all things are subjected to the *Son*, then the *Son* himself will also be subjected to the *Father*, who put all things in subjection under the Son so that the *Father* may be *all in all*."

When Jesus presents the completed kingdom to his Father, *"I am the way, the truth, and the life, no one comes to the Father but by me,"* (John 14:6) will be demonstrated to be true! Jesus is the one and only presenter of all creation to the Father! He has gathered everything to himself, whether in heaven or on earth (Ephesians 1:10). He holds the whole of creation in his hands, and he will put it all in God's hands so that God the Father will fill all!

All of God's enemies are to be destroyed. *In the end there are only two options*—life in the new creation as either a joint heir with Christ or among "the nations;" or to be destroyed prior to the arrival of the new creation when death and evil are destroyed. When this world passes away, so will death, sin, evil, and all manner of violence and suffering. Jesus' future is to free this world from these powers. This is the joy that Jesus anticipated that enabled him to endure the cross. There will be no more survival of the strong and death for the weak in the world to come.

There will be no more predators when the wolf and the lamb lie down together in the new creation.

This is almost unimaginable to us. But for those of us who've experienced a foretaste of God's love, all things are possible! We can pray for the mind of Christ and imagine the joy to come. We can imagine God's love reaching from the deepest darkness to the farthest star. We can imagine an ocean of love flowing from the Son to his Father and the Father to his Son. And that same love poured out upon us through the Holy Spirit. We can imagine the great joy that will be the Son's when he places the kingdom in his Father's hands. We can imagine the great joy that will be the Father's when He receives the kingdom from his Son.

We can imagine the joy that will be our Lord's when God comes to dwell among us. We can imagine the gratitude that the Father must feel for his Son's love of us and his creation. We can imagine the gratitude the Son must feel for God's raising him from the dead and making him Lord. We can imagine the joy we will feel when we are seated beside him on his throne. We can imagine the joy that will be ours when the Holy Spirit enables us to extend God's mercy and healing to the nations. We can imagine the gratitude the nations will feel as they receive life and healing from the servants of God. We can imagine the meaning this will bring to our lives. We can imagine the joy that will be ours when we realize that God has fulfilled his purpose for us and that we've fulfilled ours for him. We praise God for revealing these things ahead of time. We rejoice with those who can rejoice with us in the discovery of this missing gospel!

13

RAPTURE ROBBERY

Though church's failure to grasp the vision that brought the joy that enabled Jesus to endure the cross allowed belief in the rapture to gain traction.

This plus our locating the kingdom of heaven somewhere beyond this world opened the door for many to expect the total destruction of this world. They believe that only those snatched away in the rapture or converted during the seven years of tribulation will be spared. They expect the destruction of the rest of humanity and the world. Most expect the end of the world to happen in a nuclear exchange. Thankfully the gospel proclaims a better hope than this.

The church has always understood the Creator and Redeemer to be one God. They are one with each other. If we picture God the Father as the Creator and the Son as the Redeemer, they're still one and the same Lord. Jesus said, "Whoever has seen me has seen the Father" (John 14:9). John 6:38 reads, "For I have come down from heaven, not to do my own will, but the will of him who sent me." John 3:17 declares, "Indeed, God did not send the Son into the world to condemn the world, but in order that the world would be saved through him."

God's condemnation would mean the world's destruction. God did not send Jesus the Redeemer to rapture some and destroy the rest of the human race. Jesus doing so would be a violation of God's will! God and the Son would then be in a conflicted relationship. Alienation would take place in God, which is a ridiculous thought. *This would rob Jesus of the joy set before him on his way to the cross. The loss of the majority of humankind and the destruction of the world bringing joy to Jesus is a blasphemous thought! The Son's future is to first judge and then reign with us when this world is transformed by God's new creation.*

Millions expect the rapture of the church prior to the destruction of the world. Paul warned against "shifting from the hope promised by the gospel" (Colossians 1:23). Paul would see hope for the rapture as shifting away from his gospel. Paul never mentions the rapture and would have never allowed anyone to proclaim such a hope in his name. The word *rapture* or its equivalent is not found in the Bible.

Rapture proponents misinterpret 1 Thessalonians 4:16–17, which states, "For the Lord himself, with a cry of command, with the archangels call and with the sound of God's trumpet, will descend from heaven, and the dead in Christ will rise first. Then we who are alive, who are left, will be caught up in the clouds together with them to meet the Lord in the air, and so we will be with the Lord forever." These are key verses for those who seek to make Paul a teacher of the rapture. *But these verses are about resurrection, not rapture.* Paul wrote to respond to some in the church who were afraid that those who had died before Christ's return would not be resurrected with those who are alive. Paul writes to assure them that they would all be resurrected together when Christ returns. Clouds in this passage are a metaphor for the presence of God. A thick cloud descends on Mount Sinai when God speaks to Moses. God speaks from a cloud on the mount of transfiguration. The word Paul uses for meeting refers to the practice of a group of citizens going out to meet a dignitary, not to turn around and go back to the city he came from. It was to escort him into their city. Jesus coming to meet the church in the air and then turning around and taking them all back to heaven is not found in the Bible. Rapture is often substituted for resurrection in the writings of those who are promoting the rapture.

Rapture theologians usually teach that an end-time war in the Holy Land is inevitable. There is nothing we can do about it. We are to hope and pray for this since this is necessary before Christ can return the second time and set up his kingdom. But it's the peacemakers that Jesus called the children of God, not those who baptize war (Matthew 5:9). If God is going to destroy both the world and our enemies, then why should we "love our enemies and pray for those who persecute us?" (Matthew 5:44). Expecting the destruction of the world undermines our call to care for God's creation. Why should we take care of the environment if God is about to destroy it? Rapture theology leads away from our calling to follow Jesus and mature in Christlike love.

This hope jeopardizes our being enthroned with Christ. Jesus accepted God's leading to suffer on behalf of others and his world. We are called to do the same. This means we accept responsibility for our actions toward others and our world. We sacrifice for their sakes. We identify with their suffering. We don't run away from the world's suffering. We share in it. The hope that the rapture will enable us to escape suffering is incompatible with Jesus-like love.

Satan desires life for himself and death for us and our world. The destruction of as many as possible and all creation is Satan's purpose, not God's. The mass murder anticipated in rapture theology would be a victory for Satan and a loss for God. There can be no joy for Jesus in this. Who can hope for this? Could it be that the elemental spirits are leading many into bondage by distorting the gospel as was the case for the Galatians? We must ask these questions for the sake of the sheep who may be carried away by the wolves.

These issues need to be addressed by our churches in more effective ways. Even though the rapture has been rejected by almost all Protestant denominations and the Catholic church, it's widely believed in conservative fundamentalist churches. These groups dominate Christian radio and television. They provide a powerful platform for spreading their beliefs. Fundamentalist evangelists and the "Left Behind" series, which has sold more than sixty-two million books, have led millions to expect the rapture. The purpose of the kingdom amongst us and heaven when we die is to make us Christlike. The purpose of the rapture is to escape to heaven and watch while others suffer the tribulation. Our safely watching from heaven while others endure horrible suffering would be Satan-like, not Christlike.

When we examine rapture theology, we discover severe distortions of the gospel. These writers envision Christ returning twice and not once as promised in Scripture. The first time he returns secretly and snatches away all born-again Christians. In the popular fiction novels cars and planes crash because drivers and pilots just disappear. Unthinkable disasters happen across the globe. Families are always ripped apart. Some are taken. Others are left behind. Whether we are taken or left behind, who can hope for the loss of family and friends? This would mean grief for all. All of this is followed by a seven-year period of tribulation. Jesus does not become Lord until the end of the tribulation. Thus, they deny the New Testament witness that Jesus Christ is already Lord. The fact that Jesus is Lord has always been a basic teaching of the church. But according to Rev. John Hague and other megachurch leaders, the Devil is currently Lord in our world.

The countdown to Armageddon began with the establishment of the state of Israel, according to Hal Lindsey, author of *The Late Great Planet Earth*. This was necessary before the rapture could occur. Thus, the New Testament writers and all who hoped for the return of Christ up until then hoped for an impossibility. The nation of Israel must now reclaim all of its original land and rebuild the temple on its original site before the rapture. This will require either moving the Dome of the Rock or its destruction. Israel doing either would surely mean war, as this is the third holiest site for Muslims. When Russia invades Israel, the rapture of born-again Christians occurs. The seven years of tribulation begins when the Antichrist signs a seven-year peace treaty with Israel. He breaks the treaty in three and a half years and destroys the temple that will have been rebuilt. After the tribulation Jesus returns for the second time with his saints and wins the battle of Armageddon. He reigns with them for one thousand years. Then the judgment and the world's destruction come. God's eternal kingdom arrives after the world is consumed in flames. This brief sketch of the key events presented by the promoters of the rapture is enough to cause us to ask, "How can they know all of this?" If the book of Revelation's primary purpose is to disclose what is to take place in our time, what meaning could it have had for those to whom it was written?

The claim is all of this can be found in Scripture. But this is only possible if Scripture is made to say what it does not mean. All of this is built on the assumption that God has disclosed this detailed future ahead of time in the books of Revelation and Daniel. These events must happen because God has said they will. God is not free to change any of this. God becomes the prisoner of their interpretations of Scripture. Here again people suffer because some know too much.

The foundation for their theological system is dispensationalism, which divides history into seven dispensations or ages. We are now in the sixth dispensation, the church age. The seventh age will include a thousand-year reign of Christ and end with the dawn of eternity. This system of thought is the creation of Rev. Robert N. Darby, who also originated the secret rapture belief. Darby brought dispensationalism to these shores from England between 1862 and 1877. He made at least five missionary journeys to New England, creating a church known as the Plymouth Brethren. Darby's earliest public presentation of his belief in a secret rapture for the born-again occurred at a conference in England in 1830. There is no mention of the rapture in any church tradition until then. The Scofield Reference Bible, which was published in 1909, included Scofield's dispensationalist comments mixed in with the text of the King James Bible. Millions of these Bibles were sold. This gave increased legitimacy to Darby's prophecy-based system. Numerous Bible schools and the Dallas Theological Seminary, which was founded in 1924, have trained hundreds of fundamentalist pastors in Darby's system.

An adequate evaluation of dispensationalism would require another book. This has already been well done by others. My chief concern is for the millions of good Christian people who have become believers in Darby's system and the rapture. In most cases, these folks are led by sincere Christian pastors. They have succeeded in creating an expectation of the second coming that has been missing in most of our mainline churches. But what if they are influenced by or have become captives of a demonic delusion? I am not saying this is the case. But I am saying it is possible.

I know a number of fine Christians who believe the rapture is gospel. They are active in church and community. They are as loving and helpful to others as any of us. They don't seem to realize that if God is willing to destroy the world and the great majority of the people living in it, Jesus can't be the world's Savior. He is the Savior of some, but how can we be certain which group we will be included in? The Devil may die in the flames, but he's able to take the creation and the majority of human beings with him. The belief that God would send the Son into the world for this may be a demonic deception.

One of the great dangers in all of this is the political influence these people enjoy. Both extreme right-wing conservatives and fundamentalist see the benefits of their uniting around numerous issues. Both groups are well funded and able to exert significant influence on domestic and foreign policy issues. This marriage of religion with politics has added to the power of both groups. Power may be the most seductive temptation of all. Persons who acquire it rarely give it up. Groups that hold it almost never give it up. People who are certain they know God's will and plan have little room to compromise. They take "my way or the highway" positions. This has contributed to the current inability of our government to successfully address critical issues. The increase in acceptance of this seriously flawed belief system is endangering all of us.

It poses a real and present danger to the Middle East peace process. These people believe that war involving Israel has been ordained by God and that it is sure to happen. Should it come, they would welcome it as another necessary event that must take place before Christ returns. This would be a fulfillment of prophecy and a sign of Jesus' immediate return. Some fundamentalists believe we are called to hasten the day of the Lord's return. Their attitude is this: "If this means a nuclear war, then bring it on."

After Jesus told them that on the day of judgment they would have to give an account for every careless word they had uttered, some of the scribes and Pharisees asked him for a sign. Jesus answered, "An evil and adulterous generation asks for a sign, but no sign will be given to it except the sign of the prophet Jonah. For just as Jonah was three days and three nights in the belly of the sea monster, so for three days and three nights the Son of Man will be in the heart of the earth" (Matthew 12:39–40). With this illustration, Jesus tells them and us that the only sign that will be given is his death and resurrection!

Recognizing the prophets of the kingdom requires discernment. Jesus said, "From the days of John the Baptist until now the kingdom of heaven has suffered violence, and the violent take it by force" (Matthew 11:12). There is an abundance of violence in the beliefs, writings, and statements of the current leaders of the rapture movement. They lay their hands on the Bible and tear from its pages bits and pieces of Scripture to win converts and sell books. The spirit is not one of submitting oneself to the Bible, humbly listening for the voice of God. It's aggressively searching its pages for verses that can be strung together to support the interpretations they already hold. They never ask what the Scripture meant to those to whom the letters were written. They have little interest in the author's purpose for writing. They're only interested in what is said about the future and what they can make the Bible mean. They ignore the words of Jesus that call us to be doers of his Word and to love and pray for our enemies. Thus, the spirit in which the gospels were written and the gospel itself gets left behind!

All of this calls us to ask what spirit is active in all of this? Can this be the work of the Holy Spirit? Did the Holy Spirit reveal truth to Rev. Darby and a handful of believers in the 1830s, a truth that up until then had been withheld from the church and its greatest theologians, men such as Saint Augustine, Saint Aquinas, Martin Luther, John Calvin, and the early church fathers? The willingness of the advocates of the rapture and Darby's system to ignore their writings and centuries of church tradition reveals a lack of respect for them and the work of the Holy Spirit in the church. A hidden hostility is present in their dismissing the insights and wisdom of the church's greatest saints.

I suspect the violence they expect when Jesus returns is a projection of the violence hidden in the hearts of many of these leaders. The celebration they are anticipating when they safely escape before the ground is soaked with blood and the creation melts in flames exposes their hearts. Paul warned us "to not let the go down on our anger less we make a place for the devil." Long-held anger becomes hate. Hate is the heartbeat of Satan. Hate rejoices when violence brings suffering. Scripture reveals Satan to be a master of quoting and twisting Scripture. When Scripture is made to justify deadly violence for us and the world and this is celebrated, can this be the leading of the Holy Spirit?

Darby's system generates fear. The fear that they or their loved ones may be left behind haunts millions. The fear that family members and friends may be left in a tormented world is inevitably present with true believers in the rapture. These fears are great motivators for persons to be sure they believe what they are told and they tithe. They need to stay up to date with the interpretation of current events by buying the latest paperbacks. Their favorite preachers urge them to send love offerings with the promise they will be used to spread the gospel. All of this has generated a great deal of power, status, and money for the leaders of this movement. If the demonic is especially active in all of this, I imagine Satan is doing all he can to help spread their beliefs.

It's ironic that an absence of the fear of God is so evident in the leaders who are responsible for generating so much fear. They fearlessly dismiss verses that contradict their interpretations. They sell novels that are pure fantasy as if they were honest interpretations of Scripture. Revelation's "Lamb of God" is made to be a lion eager to devour those who are not born again. They manipulate Scripture and people without concern for the account they will one day give for their ministry. They set beliefs in concrete, standing on them regardless of any contradicting evidence. Some align themselves with fanatical groups that advocate extreme measures against the government, Muslims, the United Nations, and others. According to their vision, the majority of people and nations must perish. There are obvious dangers for the church, the nation, and the world if we fail to win people to a better hope than this.

Thankfully we can choose our hope. And choose we must if we are to love. The loss of hope for others and our world displayed by advocates of the rapture reveals a loss of love. Who loves without hoping for the beloved? Because we love our children, we have hopes for them. We hope for good things, not their death and destruction. Our hope for them is evidence of our love for them. Both are true because "faith, hope, and love abide" (1 Corinthians 13:13). These three abide in relationship with each other. One affects all. If hope is lost, faith grows weak and dies. If faith in Christ is lost, hope for his coming dies on the spot. If both faith and hope fail, love's foundation crumbles.

Hope for the rapture is not reconcilable with hope for the coming kingdom. With the coming of the kingdom, death itself passes away. With the coming of the kingdom, sin and evil come to their end. The very things we assume will always be there pass away with the coming of the kingdom. The rapture of just the born-again would leave this world and the left behind in the hands of all three of these.

If our hope is reduced to heaven for the born-again, we leave the creation and unbelievers without hope. If we choose the New Testament hope, we have hope for heaven and his kingdom on earth plus the possibility of salvation for anyone. All things become possible if our hope is in the one who said, "See, I am making all things new" (Revelation 21:5).

14

HOPE FELLOWSHIPS

Hope for the coming kingdom means we expect the return of Jesus Christ. Since so many have reduced the gospel to accepting Jesus and going to heaven when we die, the hope for Christ's return has all but disappeared in many denominations. It's mainly kept alive in fundamentalist churches and groups on the margins of Christianity. So the question is this: How might we renew hope for the Lord's return? How might this critically important dimension of the gospel be saved? How might it become living bread, feeding the church once again?

Leaving ordinary life to await the Lord's return will not achieve this. Instead the expectation of his return will simply be ridiculed as will any who adopt this strategy. History is filled with groups who've done this, and the outcome is always the same. They are disappointed and the critics are proved right. Therefore, any attempt to rebuild this hope must not include turning our backs on life, setting dates or time lines, or proclaiming any signs whatsoever. These things always undermine hope for the Lord's return. Jesus said his return would be like a thief in the night. He will come when he is least expected.

I believe the way forward lies in turning our eyes on his resurrection. In Jesus' resurrection, God has done a totally new thing. God the Father raised Jesus from the dead and gave him the first resurrected body. Jesus said, "I can do nothing on my own" (John 5: 30). According to John's gospel, Jesus declared what he heard from his Father and did what He saw Him doing. *When Jesus declared that following his death he would rise again, he was proclaiming what he first heard from his Father! With Jesus' resurrection, God proved to be faithful to his promise!*

With his ascension, God has placed all things under his feet. God has promised Jesus that he will rule in his coming kingdom. God will not break his promise to his Son, whom he's already made Lord. Neither will he abandon his kingdom, which is already present with us. God's faithfulness to Jesus is certain. Therefore, so is Jesus' return and the new creation. Since they are God's promises to Jesus and this world, they are unshakable. They are certain to be realized. Proclaiming this would be new news and good news for many.

Hope is both a choice and a struggle. We hope against hope. We do this because the already present kingdom is hidden underneath our death-dominated world. Hope needs community, but sin isolates us. Suffering ceases our joy and carries it away. Our kinship to Jesus remains a hidden treasure. The darkness keeps our coming glory out of sight. The darkness has not overcome the light, but it has hidden it. Love ultimately delivers us into the hands of grief. Sorrow can overwhelm us as it did my father. Crushed dreams lead to shattered lives. Hope in ourselves sets us up for despair. We need a hope that can't be shaken. Bearing personal crosses is unsustainable apart from hope.

The return of Jesus is certain. When is a mystery. Our failure to proclaim and nurture hope for his return has left us with many who hear the Word but few who do anything about it. Hope must battle with the principalities and powers that seek its death. To live, hope in the kingdom must have legs that follow Jesus in spite of today's realities. Hope does not just sit and wait. To do so risks giving its power away. If we resign ourselves to what is, we risk becoming forgiven slaves. Resignation crucifies hope in Jesus.

Our call is to follow Jesus. This means our call is to action. Our call is to practice faith, hope, and love within our faith communities and in the world. All three involve both decision and action. Our call is to share in the mission of the church. The church's call applies to every church everywhere. The church's call is to proclaim and bear witness to the gospel. The church is called to create meaningful fellowships that edify its members. The church is called to work for peace. Our call is to help shape our world in the likeness of the coming kingdom. No corner of life will be left out of the kingdom.

Thus, the church is called to responsible care of the environment. This means our engagement with every aspect of life, including politics. Salvation means more than forgiveness now and heaven when we die. Salvation means more than our individual reconciliation with God. It means more than our becoming the righteousness of God (2 Corinthians 5:21). It means more than our being made holy as Christ is holy. Salvation means the world also becomes holy (2 Corinthians 5:19). Both the individual and the world become holy with the coming new creation!

It's certain that justice will roll down like mighty waters. The wolf will lay down with the lamb. There will be no more decay and death. The leaves of the trees by the river of life will heal the nations. There shall be no more accursed, for God himself will wipe away every tear from every eye. God himself will dwell with us. All of this is certain because God's promises to Jesus are unshakable.

As surely as heaven is holy, the kingdom of God on earth will be holy. As Jesus is holy, the saints who persevere and rule with him will also be holy. Hebrews 13:28 reads, "Therefore, since we are receiving a kingdom that cannot be shaken, let us give thanks by which we offer to God an acceptable worship with reverence and awe." Our receiving this kingdom is certain because God's promises to Jesus and the world are unshakable.

Our problem is that God has made these great promises but we go on as before as if nothing has happened. God's holiness means he is faithful to keep his Word. He has shown himself faithful to Jesus. He has shown himself faithful to the coming kingdom by its presence already among us. His righteousness is displayed in his faithfulness. What can justify our giving up hope for the return of Jesus and the coming of the kingdom of God? What reason can we give for our silence? What has brought about this failure of hope? Why are we not asking ourselves these questions?

Attempting an adequate answer to all of these questions is beyond the scope of this book. This book will have succeeded if some begin to ask questions like these. The fact that these kinds of questions are rarely raised in most of our denominations is part of the problem. This has led to the loss of the churches "ears to hear." After speaking Jesus often said: "let anyone who has ears to hear, hear". I am very aware that there is little listening for this hope in the church. Very few have ears that are ready to hear this hope as the gospel!

Institutional churches tend to become ingrown. A great deal of energy is expended in maintaining the institution. Along with bringing persons to Christ, preserving the institution becomes a high priority. Security typically becomes the top priority for human institutions. Taking seriously the return of Jesus and the coming kingdom means ; "Here we have no lasting city, but we are looking for the city that is to come" (Hebrews 13:14). When the church seeks to become a lasting city it no longer looks for the city that is to come. It no longer "waits for it with patience" (Romans 8: 25).

Following Jesus means setting the same hope before us that enabled him to endure the cross! We are called to adopt his hope for the kingdom of God on earth! This does not mean we hope for a part in handing the completed kingdom to his Father. This Jesus will do. But it does mean that we hope for his return and the transformation of creation. It means we expect to be fellow heirs with him of all things. It means we expect our resurrection. It means we expect to become kings and priests in the kingdom of God on earth. It means we expect to share in judging the world and angels (1 Corinthians 6:2–3). It means we envision this future and we receive the joy this hope can bring.

The Holy Spirit's priority is to create a Christian community. This is demonstrated in the ministry of the apostles and the early church. The Holy Spirit seeks to build Spirit-filled communities that are able to share each other's burdens as we follow Jesus—fellowships where the gifts of the Holy Spirit are expressed through every person, fellowships where it is possible to speak the truth in love to one another, fellowships committed to helping each other discern God's call in the midst of the complexities of life. This requires safe, intimate, and disciplined fellowships. A common vision and purpose is normally needed to sustain small groups. The expectation of Jesus' return and the coming kingdom can provide the vision. The purpose can be our maturing in Christ.

A shared vision and purpose based on the gospel of the coming kingdom is generally missing in the institutional church. Thus, opportunities to participate in disciplined small groups that share this vision is also missing. Since so many know so little about God's vision for his world, in many instances it will be best to begin by creating short-term hope fellowships—groups whose purpose is to explore biblical hope. Doing so will lead to many of the issues we've explored in this book. Many will treasure the hopes they discover. They will be better equipped to offer reasons for the hope they hold. And many will discover the healing power of effectively led small groups.

Thus, the church will be strengthen in its primary mission to preach and teach the gospel. If I were to return to the pastoral ministry, I would make this a high priority. Paul in Romans 1:10 declared, "I am not ashamed of the gospel: it is the power of God for salvation for everyone who has faith, to the Jew first and also the Greek."

Many of our churches have kept Jesus' return under wraps. It seems to have become an embarrassment for some. Where this is the case, our call is to repent and unashamedly preach the whole gospel. The whole gospel is immeasurable better news that the half of loaf most have been fed.

In some situations the house church model may be better suited for the creation of hope fellowships than a local church. But there is no reason that it should be either one or the other. Both have their place. They can and should support each other. Both will be strengthened when this is the case. Sometimes pastors are wary of small groups. Whether in homes or at church, the possibility of their becoming destructive is always there. But secure pastors will assume the risk and be faithful to their responsibility to serve those who believe in the need for supportive fellowships that are committed to being "doers of the word and not hearers only" (Matthew 8: 24–27).

Our place in the kingdom may be determined by which group we belong in. If we persevere in doing his Word, we will reign on a throne with Jesus. If not, we may not. Our Lord will decide. Few can persevere in this culture without the support of a community that seeks to be led by the Holy Spirit. Providing this is the call of the church.

Sharing Jesus' throne is won by sharing his suffering. We need the support of fellow pilgrims through the challenges that await all who follow Jesus. To put it crudely, our throne is not a cheap seat. It's a costly prize—a golden throne far more valuable than we can conceive.

15

WHAT REWARD DO YOU HAVE?

Hear the good news:

> You have heard it said, "you shall love your neighbor and hate your enemy." But I say to you, love your enemies and pray for those who persecute you, so that you may be children of your father in heaven; for he makes his sun rise on the evil and on the good, and sends rain on the righteousness and the unrighteous. For if you love those who love you, what reward do you have? Do not even the tax collectors do the same? And if you greet only your brothers and sisters, what more are you doing than others? Do not even the gentiles do the same? *Be perfect, therefore, as your heavenly father is perfect.* (Matthew 5:43–48).

These words strike many of us like a sledgehammer. It's hard to hear these words as good news. We hear them as demanding an impossibility. And in our own strength, that is clearly the case. But Jesus never intended that we love everyone in our own strength. But he did mean for us to be doers of his Word. He did intend that we live this out. He knew, as we know, that we cannot self-generate love of our enemies. Alone, it is impossible. But in Christ all things are possible, including loving as God loves.

These words surely shocked the crowd that first heard them. For generations the Jews had been a conquered people, suffering whatever cruelties their Roman occupiers decided to inflict. The Romans were hated with a vengeance that is hard for most of us to imagine. Many were taxed to the point of losing ownership of their land. Self-proclaimed messiahs led several revolts that ended in bloody defeats. The zealots hated the Sadducees for cooperating with the Romans. The Sadducees hated the zealots for bringing so much suffering upon them and the people. The general population hated King Herod and his sons for the suffering they inflicted upon the population. Everywhere a burning hatred that many felt was justified smoldered just under the surface. Jesus speaking these words into that atmosphere must have stunned everyone. Matthew says the crowds were *astounded* at his teaching (Matthew 7:28).

This surely shocked his disciples as well. They could hardly have felt more able to love their enemies than we do. In the same sermon they heard Jesus declare a disaster would come upon everyone who hears his words but fails to do them (Matthew 7:24–27). This didn't sound like good news to them either. But Jesus knew that he would soon be living in them and they in him. He knew that the Holy Spirit would bring the power they needed to mature in his likeness. Philip once said to him, "Lord, show us the father, and we will be satisfied." Jesus said to him, "Have I been with you all this time, Philip, and you still do not know me? Whoever has seen me has seen the Father. How can you say, 'Show us the Father?' Do you not believe that I am in the Father and the Father is in me?" (John 14:8–10).

Over and over Jesus told them that he and the Father were one. To see him is to see the Father. Thus, when he called them to be perfect as their heavenly Father is perfect, he was calling them to be like him. He was calling them to oneness with himself and the Father—a oneness that the Holy Spirit would lead them into. When we recognize that the power of the Holy Spirit provides the means for us to achieve this, we can hear this as good news. When seen through the lens of God's power and love for us, this becomes possible.

Romans 6:29 reads, "For those whom he foreknew he also predestined to be conformed to the image of his son, in order that he might be the firstborn within a large family." With this Scripture and many of those we've already cited, Paul affirms God's commitment to our becoming Christlike. Jesus and Paul sharing the same vision is exciting. This shows that Paul had the mind of Christ. Paul's becoming Christlike is seen in his words and deeds. What Paul achieved is possible for all those God has chosen to be brothers and sisters of Jesus.

To share this vision, we need to understand that Jesus could not have said, "Be perfect." There was no such word in either the Aramaic or Hebrew languages. The word used by Matthew is *teleios*. It is a Greek aesthetic term used in describing art or sculpture. It was not used to describe persons since the Greeks viewed being perfect as unattainable by human beings.

Luke 6:36 reads, "Be merciful, just as your father is merciful." This is a much better rendering of Jesus' meaning. This echoes Leviticus 19:2, which reads, "Be holy, for I the Lord your God am holy." The Hebrew word *tamim* is used in Deuteronomy 18:13. There it means whole or complete or to have integrity. Matthew may have substituted *teleios* for *tamim*. In this paragraph Jesus calls us to act as God acts. This means we are to love everyone, even our enemies. Ours is to be an all-inclusive love just as God's love includes all. Obeying Jesus means we give up our futile attempts to be perfect and commit ourselves to an all-inclusive love. This requires that we give ourselves wholly to God. It's solely by grace through faith that this becomes achievable.

Since our being conformed to the likeness of Christ is God's goal for us, we can count on him to supply the grace needed for us to achieve this. It's probably safe to say that few have achieved this. I doubt very many are committed to this. Arriving at wholeness and holiness can only be achieved with great effort, usually over many years. But there are those who've made the effort, and probably more than we might think have reached maturity in Christ.

Dr. Martin Luther King, Sr., was one whom I believe achieved this. While I was serving as an associate pastor at Peachtree Road United Methodist Church in Atlanta, Dr. King preached a noontime sermon during Holy Week. This was a little more than a year after his wife and one of his church members had been shot and killed by a deranged person during worship. This tragedy took place a year or so after Dr. Martin Luther King, Jr., was assassinated in Memphis.

Near the end of his sermon Dr. King declared, "I'll not give any man the power to make me hate." Along with those words there came a flood of love unlike anything I've ever experienced in worship. Heart-cleansing love poured over the congregation, washing us in the Holy Spirit of the Lamb. I was privileged to witness the fruits of God's amazing grace that had brought one who had suffered such senseless tragedies to be a bearer of Spirit-matured love. Based on this experience and my friendships with a few people who seem to have achieved this, I'm convinced that becoming Christlike in this life is achievable. No doubt there are numerous reasons for so many Christians to fall far short of this ideal. Five of the more obvious reasons include the following:

1. Few make this their goal, and many of those who do end up turning back when they discover how hard this process will be and what it will cost. Those whom God calls, *he calls to come and die to self.* This is more than just a one-time event. This is an ongoing process for those who "forgetting what lies behind press on to this high calling in Christ Jesus."

2. Few have a safe, supportive Christian fellowship where deep sharing is possible and this degree of love is sought. Without such support, enduring the suffering that comes to the followers of Jesus is often unsustainable.

3. Few hope to become kings and priests in the coming new creation. Few realize that maturing in Christlike love is necessary for serving with Jesus on his throne. Many have assumed that simply going to heaven is the goal. They have not heard the whole gospel preached or taught. Thus, they are unaware of God's ultimate salvation and our role in the coming kingdom. They assume that their having faith in Christ is all that is asked of them. Some even believe that their working toward maturity would amount to an attempt to be saved by works and cause them to lose their salvation.

4. Few persist in praying for wholeness and holiness.

5. Some may suffer genetic diseases, birth defects, or early deaths that prevent their achieving Christlike wholeness in this life. Jesus did not have bipolar disorder, but I do. So far my earlier doubts about my achieving perfection in this life have been confirmed. My death will mean the death of my bipolar disorder. I believe every imperfect believer will receive healing, wholeness, and holiness in heaven.

This journey to wholeness and holiness in Christ is never completed overnight. Whether one's life is long or short, this is a lifetime process for all those who would seek to be conformed to the image of Christ. Through the grace of God the Holy Spirit provides all that is impossible for us. The Spirit leads us to see our part in the process. Step by step, the Holy Spirit supplies the power for us to overcome our sins and temptations.

Learning to love one's enemies begins with a decision to make this our goal. When we consider this, we are likely to discover that we really don't want to do this. There are people out there we don't want to love. They've hurt us too deeply. Making this decision means *being willing to be made willing*. When this is not what we want, we need to pray and ask for our next step in changing our desires. We need to pray for guidance and expect the Spirits direction. Our next step will often be to forgive those we really don't want to forgive. Where this is the case, first deciding and then acting is the means toward changing our feelings. Where the hurt is deep, this usually means repeating this process numerous times. *It often requires our acting as if we've forgiven them before we have!* If we wait until we feel like forgiving, we'll never forgive them. Persistent "acting as if" will bring the change the Spirit is at work to create in us. Hope "acts as if" in spite of the circumstances and our feelings. Dr. King had to choose to forgive those who murdered his wife, son, and church member. Feelings provide the energy for doing amazing things. Dr. King employed the energy in his hurt and anger against the forces that tempted him to hate. Hate is the natural fruit of long-held anger. If you hold on to your anger long enough, the temptation to hate will follow. Dr. King chose to forgive and not hate. The Holy Spirit worked with him to fill him with the love that poured out on us that day.

I want to be that kind of man. I'm not there yet; however, I've seen it in others, and I know that love even for our enemies is possible. Jesus assures us that this is the will of God for us. Our part is simply to discern the small and large decisions and actions we must take to contribute to the process.

Ten years after World War II a group of Polish Christians in Warsaw were asked if they would be willing to meet with a group of West German Christians. They wanted to ask for forgiveness for what Germany had done to Poland during the war. There was silence at first, and then someone said with great feeling, "Each stone in Warsaw is soaked in Polish blood! We cannot forgive! What you are asking is impossible!" Later that evening someone suggested that they close their meeting with the Lord's Prayer. Everyone agreed, but as they prayed, "Forgive us our sins as we forgive," they stopped in mid-sentence. They sat in silence for a time. Then the man who had spoken out so strongly softly said, "I must say yes to you. I could no more pray the Our Father or call myself a Christian if I refuse to forgive. Humanly speaking, I cannot do it. But God will give us the strength." A year and a half later Polish and West German Christians met in Vienna and began a lasting fellowship. No action is more likely to lead to a miracle than our forgiving our enemies!

If we are to rule with Jesus in the coming kingdom, we must love our enemies! This is the acid test we must pass if we are to rule from Jesus' throne! Our ruling with him as kings and priests is at stake in our doing … or not doing his Word! In Revelation the nations are the enemies of God. Ruling them along with Jesus means ruling in the power of his enemy-loving love. If we are to be their priests, representing them to God and bringing them to him, we must do so in Jesus-like love. The chief purpose of our learning to love our enemies is to prepare us to serve the nations as rulers and priests in the coming kingdom.

Sharing his throne is the reward Jesus has in mind in Matthew 5:46. What a great reward! Those who mature in Christlike love of enemies will rule with Jesus. Jesus asking, "If you love those who love you, what reward do you have?" suggests there is no reward for loving like everybody else! But there is a great reward for loving like God loves!

Jesus promises the disciples a place on his throne when the renewal of all things occurs (Matthew 19:27–28). This Scripture reads, "Then Peter said in reply, 'Look we have left everything and followed you. What then will we have?' Jesus said to them, 'Truly I tell you, at the renewal of all things, when the Son of Man is seated on the throne of his glory, you who have followed me will also sit on twelve thrones, judging the twelve tribes of Israel."

Since the majority of Christians appear to never achieve the goal of an all-inclusive love, we may hope to achieve this in heaven. I believe that heaven's great purpose is to continue preparing us for our place in the coming kingdom. If so, then learning to love like Jesus is at the heart of heaven's work. Since this would be consistent with God's purpose, I believe this is possible. For my own and most of my family and friends' sakes, I certainly hope so. But since this is not clearly promised in Scripture, this may not be the case. Or this may only be possible for those who begin maturing here through the work of repentance.

I know a lady who loves her job putting together a newspaper so much that she often says, "I hope there is a newspaper for me to work on in heaven." I doubt she'll find one there. But I do expect that her unique gifts and talents will find a place of service in God's kingdom. It could be that there will be other ways of serving other than acting as kings and priests in the coming kingdom. If so, heaven may enhance those gifts and talents for a variety of services not mentioned in Scripture. All of our questions aren't answered in Scripture. But the Bible does tell us all we need to know, believe, and do to become joint heirs with Christ of all things!

16

OUR ESSENTIAL WEAPON

The doers of Jesus' Word are promised a throne. When we understand what is asked of us, the question becomes this: "How do we acquire the power to do his Word?" The internal and external forces opposed to us will defeat all who deceive themselves into believing they can do this alone. This is only possible for those who make this journey trusting our Lord. Prayer is the means of our receiving the power needed to be doers of his Word. Prayer is an essential weapon in our struggle to become joint heirs with Christ.

Prayer brings the power of God into our journey. Only those who persist in prayer become priests in God's kingdom. The lives of saints like Dr. King bear witness to the power of prayer. Jesus is our final authority on the power of prayer. He declared that "everyone who asks receives, and everyone who searches finds, and for everyone who knocks, the door will be opened" (Matthew 7:8). He based his confidence in prayer on his perception of the compassion and power of God (Matthew 7:11).

Jesus' astonishing belief in the power of prayer is displayed in his teaching his disciples to pray, "Thy kingdom come, thy will be done, on earth as it is in heaven." *Jesus would not have taught his disciples a meaningless prayer! His teaching them to pray these words shows that he believed their doing so would impact the coming of God's kingdom! If this were not so, he would not have taught them to pray this way. Since our prayers affect the coming of the kingdom, what limit can we impose on the power of prayer? When we view the power of prayer through Jesus' eyes, prayer is shown to be our most powerful weapon in our struggle to be doers of his Word!*

We need to remember that the coming of the kingdom of God on earth and the arrival of the new creation are separate events. Jesus taught his disciples to pray for the coming of God's kingdom. He never called them to pray for the coming new creation. He understood that the new creation would be brought about by his Father apart from any human involvement.

When people are faced with difficult situations, we often hear them say, "There is nothing we can do but pray." The feelings that usually accompany these words include helplessness and resignation. The implication is that prayer is at the bottom of the list of things that can be done to impact the situation.

But Jesus knows more about the power of prayer than we do! If we accept that and adopt his view of prayer, we will give prayer the respect it deserves. Adopting his understanding of the power and promise of prayer is essential if we are to win a place on his throne. Prayer is our great weapon against all the forces aligned in opposition to the coming of God's kingdom. Scripture presents both prayer and sharing the sufferings of Christ as impacting the coming kingdom. Prayer calls down the power necessary to bear our share of Christ's suffering. Discovering our way to effective prayer must be a top priority. Being conformed to the image of our Lord requires passionate and persistent prayer. The price to be paid in time and effort cannot be compared with our reigning as kings in the coming new creation.

Our prayers affect what happens in heaven, and heaven impacts what happens on earth. This is powerfully illustrated in the vision John describes in chapters 5 through 8 of Revelation. John sees Jesus standing as a lamb before the throne of God. John begins to weep because no one could be found to open God's scroll and break its seals. John's weeping ends when he is told that the lion of the tribe of Judah has conquered and that he can open the scroll (Revelation 5: 5). When the fifth seal is broken, heaven's martyred witnesses cry out, "Sovereign Lord, holy and true, how long will it be before you judge and avenge our blood on the inhabitants of the earth?" They were given white robes and told to rest a little longer *until the number would be complete both of their fellow servants and of their brothers and sisters who were soon to be killed(Revelation 6: 10-11).* When the sixth seal is broken, the whole of creation shakes and staggers in anticipation of the coming of God's wrath. Before the seventh seal is opened, the saved are marked out for a new Passover.

When the seventh seal is broken, heaven's ceaseless praise is broken, and there's silence in heaven for about thirty minutes. An angel with a golden censer is given a great quantity of incense to offer with the prayers of the saints. Silently God breathes in the sweet-smelling prayers of his people. Heaven's endless praise has been interrupted so that God may hear even the softest prayer. The silence is broken when one by one the trumpets are sounded and the wrath that proceeds the coming of the kingdom breaks out on earth. John's heavenly vision pictures our prayers as having an impact both in heaven and on earth. The prayers of mere mortals alter life in heaven. John's experience is another conformation of Jesus' view of the power of prayer.

Prayer is difficult! Passionate and persistent prayer is hard work! It's a struggle to persist in praying, especially so when there is no evidence of our prayers making any difference. The only time most of us pray for the coming of God's kingdom is when we pray the Lord's Prayer. This is not something very many are pressing God for. Jesus did not intend for us to pray the prayer he taught and then move on to praying for the really important things. Jesus sees God's kingdom as more important than all the rest. He made this clear when he said, "But strive first for the kingdom of God and his righteousness, and all these things will be given to you as well" (Matthew 6:33).

After he fasted and mourned for three weeks, Daniel saw a man in a vision. When he heard the sound of his words, he fell into a trance with his face to the ground.

> But then a hand touched me and roused me to my hands and knees. He said to me, "Daniel, greatly beloved, pay attention to the words that I am going to speak to you. Stand on your feet, for I have now been sent to you." So while he was speaking this word to me, I stood trembling. He said to me: "Do not fear, Daniel, for from the first day that you set your mind to gain understanding and to humble yourself before your God, your words have been heard, and I have come because of your words. But the prince of the kingdom of Persia, opposed me twenty one days. So Michael, one of the chief princes came to help me, and I left him there with the prince of the kingdom of Persia, and have come to help you understand what is to happen to your people at the end of days. For there is a further vision for those days." (Daniel 10:10–14)

Here for the first time the Bible reveals a warfare taking place in the spiritual world that blocks the answer to prayer! Daniel was heard the first day he prayed. But "the prince of the kingdom of Persia" prevented his prayer from being answered for twenty-one days. When the prayers of believers seemingly go unanswered, we usually conclude one of the following: Either we didn't have enough faith, or we prayed doubting as James describes (James 1:6–7), or, God said no, or wait, or it was just not his will. Thus, people usually end up either blaming themselves or attributing unanswered prayer to God. The possibility that the cause was none of the above but rather the result of a struggle in the spiritual world never enters our minds! So people end up blaming themselves or God while the Devil applauds!

Daniel had to persevere for twenty-one days to receive an answer to his prayer. Jesus may have had this warfare in the unseen world in mind when immediately after he taught them the Lord's Prayer, he told the story found in Luke 11:5–8. This Scripture emphasizes the need for persisting in prayer.

This thread of persistent prayer runs throughout the Old Testament. When Abraham learned that Yahweh was about to destroy Sodom, where his nephew, Lot, lived with his wife and two daughters, he began a struggle for their lives. Genesis 18:16–33 records the give-and-take as Abraham sought to intercede with God to rescue them. He appeals to God's righteousness by saying, "Will you indeed sweep away the righteous with the wicked? Suppose there are fifty righteous within the city; will you then sweep away the place and not forgive it for the fifty righteous who are in it?" When the Lord relented and promised to spare the city if fifty righteous could be found, Abraham asked if he would spare the city if forty-five could be found. When God accepted this number, Abraham asked if forty and then thirty and then twenty and finally ten would be enough to spare the city. The point is that God was responsive to Abraham's persistent haggling with him over the number needed. Upon learning of God's plan, Abraham didn't just say, "Thy will be done." He negotiates a better outcome by asking God over and over to lower the number he required.

The Lord God resolved to destroy Israel when he found them worshiping a golden calf. But Moses interceded on their behalf. He did so in spite of God's promise that he would make a great nation with Moses. Exodus 32:14 reads, "And the Lord changed his mind about the disaster that he planned to bring to his people." Moses prayer caused God to change his mind. Scripture speaks of Jacob's wrestling all night until the angel of the Lord blessed him. Martin Luther understood the necessity of persisting in prayer. He once said, "I rubbed God's ear with all of his promises about hearing prayer."

In Luke 18:2–8 Jesus told a story to illustrate the need to pray always and not to lose heart. He said, "In a certain city there was a judge who neither feared God nor had respect for people." In that city there was a widow who kept coming to him and saying, "Grant me justice against my opponent." For a while he refused, but later he said to himself, "Though I have no fear of God and no respect for anyone, yet because this widow keeps bothering me, I will grant her justice, so that she may not wear me out by continually coming." And the Lord said, "Listen to what the unjust judge says. And will not God grant justice to his chosen ones who cry to him day and night? Will he delay long in helping them? I tell you, he will quickly grant justice to them. And yet, when the Son of Man comes, will he find faith on earth?" When we align our prayers with the purposes of God we've explored in this book, this Scripture assures us that God will act quickly to help us.

Persistent prayer enables us to become doers of his Word. Doing his Word empowers our maturing in Christ. To be mature in Christ is to have the mind of Christ. If we are to rule with Christ in the coming kingdom, we must acquire the mind of Christ! Sharing his throne is for those who've matured in his likeness! There will be no conflict in thought or action among those who rule with him. We will be one with him, and he will be one with us. We will think as he thinks, love as he loves, and act as he acts. The same mind that was in Christ Jesus will be in those who serve the nations in the coming kingdom of God!

The mystery of Christ in us is the basis of our hope of sharing God's glory. Colossians 1:27–29 reads,

> To them God chose to make known how great among the Gentiles are the riches of the glory of this mystery, which is Christ in you, the hope of glory. It is he whom we proclaim, warning everyone in all wisdom, so that we may present everyone mature in Christ. For this I toil and struggle with all the energy that he powerfully inspires within me.

Paul pours all of his energy into presenting everyone mature in Christ. His great desire is to see them rule with Christ in the coming kingdom.

Maturity in Christ does not come automatically when someone becomes a Christian. Becoming a Christian begins a journey toward being conformed to the image of Christ. Paul describes the way to maturity in Christ in Colossians 3. Being conformed to the image of Christ involves a process of *putting to death* anger, wrath, malice, slander, abuse, lies, fornication, impurity, passion, evil desires, greed, and the like and *putting on* compassion, kindness, humility, meekness, patience, love, gratitude, wisdom, and the peace of Christ. This process of putting to death our destructive characteristics and putting on Christlike qualities requires our very best efforts!

The Christian journey is one of continuing repentance! Repentance is more than a one-time event. It's a lifetime of turning from the attitudes and behaviors that lead to death and turning to those that lead to wholeness and holiness. Repentance, like prayer, is a lifelong necessity. The struggle to free ourselves from our self-sabotaging behaviors inevitably leads to warfare with the principalities and powers that strive to enslave us. These forces and our resistance to dying to self fight to keep us in the death grip of sin. If repentance were solely our work, brought about by our efforts alone, we would surely fail. But we are not alone. The Holy Spirit empowers our struggle for freedom from the powers that seek our death.

In Galatians 5 Paul exhorts us to "live by the spirit." Verses 24 and 25 read, "And those who belong to Christ Jesus have crucified the flesh with its passions and desires. If we live by the Spirit, let us also be guided by the Spirit." Paul expects life in the Holy Spirit to bring an awareness of the destructive dimensions of our lives and the power to put them to death. After he lists fifteen examples of the "works of the flesh," Paul points to "the fruits of the Spirit" that repentance produces. He names "love, joy, peace, patience, kindness, generosity, faithfulness, gentleness and self-control." Repentance is putting to death the worthless that is passing away to gain the valuable that endures. Repentance is love's great gift to those God prepares to share his throne!

Philippians 1:6 reads, "I am confident of this, that the one who began a good work among you will bring it to completion by the day of Jesus Christ." Paul is confident that Jesus will produce in them "the harvest of righteousness for the glory and praise of God" (Philippians 1:11). He calls them to "let the same mind be in you that was in Christ Jesus" (Philippians 2:5). Paul expects a life of Spirit-empowered repentance to develop in us the mind of Christ!

I'm deeply grateful for the healing I've received and the maturity I've gained over my seventy-six years. But when I measure myself against the mind of Christ, my failure to mature in him is undeniable. My progress seems small. The gap to be closed is great. Acquiring the mind that was in Christ Jesus seems impossible for me in this life.

Sorrow and anxiety are the fruits that have ripened on much of my life's tree. Powerful emotional and mental dynamics that are hidden in the deep places of my heart and mind still persist in sabotaging my growth. When I come against old ingrained patterns, my repentance has often been too weak to win my freedom. This was my experience even when I was at my best before the emergence of my bipolar disorder.

Now when I face the realities of my own mind, I'm pulled toward despair. There have been too many days in darkness to be confident of my ability to see. One of the devastating realities of my bipolar disorder has been the loss of trust in myself. Not being able to trust my own thoughts has brought more pain than I have words to express. A poet is needed to give expression to the grief that abides where my basic trust once lived. I suspect that only victims of bipolar or other mental disorders can identify with the ruin that the collapse of one's mental house brings. The loss of self-trust spread anxiety to every corner of my soul. I fear the disease will return and overpower the medications that keep me well. When the disease is active, it ceases control of my mind and leads me into destructive judgments and behaviors. I live with the possibility of another emergence inflicting fresh wounds.

Sustaining the repentance that results in maturity in Christ may not be possible for me. I've certainly not achieved this up until now! I can only imagine the grief that would be mine if after I have seen the possibility of acquiring the mind of Christ, I am left with the mind I have now! This plus my failure to more effectively communicate the gospel to the living dead around me would drown me in grief!

Even though I have plenty of doubts about me, I have no doubt about him. I have no doubt that his love will be sufficient for me. How can I be so sure? It's because I've discovered that "I have an advocate with the Father, Jesus Christ the righteous!"

I'm confident that the hope I've presented in this book will not disappoint me. I believe all that remains that must be put to death will die at my death. I believe I will put on all that is lacking in my heavenly community. *Even though I've not been a doer of his word in everything, I feel assured of a place with Jesus on his throne!* I'm confident of this in spite of all my doubts. Given the realities of my life, it's right for you and me to ask, "How can I be so sure of this?" My assurance is not based on my faith, or my theology, or on any good I may have done in this life. If it were, I would lack this assurance.

My assurance is anchored in Jesus' prayer to his Father for me! We overhear Jesus praying his longest recorded prayer in John 17. Verses 20 through 26 provide all the assurance I need. My advocate prayed,

> I ask not only on behalf of these, but also on behalf of those who will believe in me through their word, that they may all be one. As you, Father, are in me and I am in you, may they also be in us, so that the world may believe that you have sent me. The glory that you have given me I have given them, so that they be one, as we are one. I in them and you in me, that they may become completely one, so that the world may know that you sent me and have loved them even as you have loved me. Father, I desire that those also

whom you have given me, may be with me where I am, to see my glory, which you have given me because you loved me before the foundation of the world. Righteous Father, the world does not know that you have sent me. I made your name known to them, and I will make it known, so that the love with which you have loved me may be in them, and I in them.

I am a member of that great body of witnesses that have been born again through trusting the New Testament writers. My believing their witness and prayer led to my receiving the Holy Spirit. This is Jesus' last prayer with his disciples before he is arrested and brought to trial. In these moments Jesus lifts us into the intimacy he shares with his Father. We hear him pour out his passionate desire for all who receive him. His deepest desire and prayer is that w*e be one with him and one with his Father!* To be one with Jesus is to be mature in him. It is to be filled with the mind of Christ. It is to have come to "fullness in him" (Colossians 2:10). Jesus asks that the love the Father has for him also reside in us! Jesus prays that we be gathered into the eternal river of love flowing from the Father to the Son ... and the Son to the Father in the power of the Holy Spirit. He asks that we be with him where he is to behold his glory. *He is praying that we be with him on his throne!* With this prayer, Jesus affirms the hope Scripture proclaims from Genesis to Revelation.

My assurance is based on God answering Jesus' prayer! It's inconceivable that God ignored this prayer or answered with a no! His prayer will be fully answered! All that Jesus asks will be granted! Everything Jesus prays for will come about! "If we are faithless, God remains faithful, for he cannot deny himself " (2 Timothy 2:13).

Life is fragile and uncertain. I may not put to death in me all that needs to die. I may not reach the holiness I expect. I may completely lose touch with reality. My faith may crumble under my feet. Many of my beliefs may miss the mark. I may be labeled a heretic by some in the church. *But I will still see him in his glory! I will become one with him and one with our Father! And so will all who believe the gospel and follow Christ! God's faithfulness is certain! The day will come when we all will shout, "Home at last, home at last. Thank God Almighty we are home at last!"*

Saint Paul wrote: "Blessed be the God and Father of our Lord Jesus Christ who has blessed us in Christ with every spiritual blessing in the heavenly places, just as he chose us in Christ before the foundation of the world to be holy and blameless before him in love" (Ephesians 1: 3).

Paul grounds our salvation in God's having chosen us before the foundation of the world. This is the reason we will inherit all things one day. This is why we will reign with Jesus. It is this event in God that has secured all of this for us. This is first and foremost grounded in God's decision, not ours.

My personal assurance is also grounded in an event that took place in God. It rests on Jesus' prayer for me, not on my faith or my born-again experience. This means I can pray both "Our Father" and "My Father." It means I can pray "Abba", "Daddy," along with all the children of God.

17

COME WALK WITH ME

We've now come to the place that we can ask: "Is there still more of the gospel bread left for us to unwrap? Is there any more of the missing gospel to be found?" Yes there is! There's still more gospel hidden under our silence. More truth to empower our journey with Jesus. To see this we need to consider Matthew 14: 22-33 which reads:

"Immediately he made the disciples get into the boat and go on ahead to the otherside, while he dismissed the crowds. And after he had dismissed the crowds, he went up the mountain by himself to pray. When evening came, he was there alone, but by this time the boat, battered by the waves, was far from land for the wind was against them. And early in the morning he came walking toward them on the sea. But when the disciples saw him walking on the sea, they were terrified, saying, "it is a ghost!" And they cried out in fear. But immediately Jesus spoke to them and said, "Take heart, it is I, do not be afraid."

Peter answered him, "Lord, if it is you, command me to come to you on the water." He said "Come." So Peter got out of the boat and started walking on the water, and came toward Jesus. But when he noticed the strong wind, he became frightened and beginning to sink, he cried out, "Lord save me!" Jesus immediately reached out his hand and caught him, saying to him, "You of little faith, why did you doubt?"

When they got into the boat, the wind ceased. And those in the boat worshiped him, saying, "Truly you are the Son of God."

We have no reason to doubt that Jesus walked on water. As in Matthew, both Mark and John report his doing so immediately after the the feeding of the five thousand. But did Peter really walk on water? Or is this a parable-like story the Holy Spirit inspired Matthew to include in his gospel? Must we assume that this really happened to see the meaning for us in this story?

Parables aren't descriptons of events that actually happened. They are stories Jesus created to help his people picture present and future realities. As with his parables, the truth to be found in this story does not depend on this event having actually happened. My personal view is Peter never got out of the boat. I believe his walking on water is an addition to the text that illustrates profound truth. Whether Peter actually got his feet wet or not is not the issue. The Spirit's ability to use this story to display the gospel is not dependent on the answer to this question.

Peter walking on water isn't reported in the other gospels or anywere else in the New Testament. Peter says nothing about this in his letters. When shipwrecked, Saint Paul didn't walk to shore. It's hard for me to imagine that this could have happened and remain unmentioned in the rest of the New Testament.

Jesus created parables to teach his disciples and us. Like Jesus' parables, we are invited to imagine this as a real event and to picture ourselves in the boat with the disciples. Assuming this really did happen will enable the story to speak to us. This is the Holy Spirit's purpose for the story. So let's imagine our putting together a power point presentation of this event. A power point presentation will help us see another slice of the gospel's missing bread.

Let's begin with a picture of the disciples laboring to row the boat in the darkness of early morning. Next we see Jesus coming toward them walking on the rough seas of that stormy morning. At first they think he is a ghost. They are terrified. We see them crying out in fear. Next, we see Jesus responding. We hear him say; "Take heart, it is I; do not be afraid."

Then we see Peter standing in the boat calling out to Jesus. We hear him say; "Lord, if it is you, command me to come to you on the water." Let's take another snap shot of this scene. The waves are churning, the boat is rocking, as this big fishermen stands with his eyes fixed on Jesus.

Let's pause here and ask, "Why did Peter ask Jesus to do this?" The text suggests that Peter is testing Jesus. If so, then what did he expect to learn if Jesus says "come walk with me?" What would that have meant to Peter and the disciples?

To answer these questions we need to recall Jesus sending his disciples out to "the lost sheep of the house of Israel." Matthew reports this in chapter 10 of his gospel. Jesus tells them to; "proclaim the good news of the nearness of the kingdom of heaven, and cure the sick, raise the dead, cleanse the lepers, and cast out demons." Matthew placing this prior to Peter walking on water is significant. The memory of all these things happening was powerfully present with Peter when he called out to Jesus. That very day they had fed 5,000 men plus woman and children with just five loaves and two fish! What impact did their doing these things, especially raising the dead, have on the disciples? All of this must have left them needing to know what they could and could not do. This is what Peter wants to know. His question is, "If we trust you, will we be able to continue doing all the things that you are doing?" Knowing his thoughts, and desiring to show him that this will soon be true, Jesus says; "Come."

Our next slide shows Jesus answering with a broad smile on his face. Jesus knows and in John's gospel he tells them that when the Holy Spirit comes they will do even greater things than he is doing. In part to have them see that this will soon be so, Jesus says "Come." This did not mean they would be able to walk on water as they went about their ministry. This was either self-evident or quickly demonstrated after Pentecost. There's no record of any of the disciples ever attempting to walk on water after Pentecost. But Peter's question wasn't the primary reason Jesus responded as he did. I can see Jesus as being willing to affirm their future Holy Spirit- empowered ministry. However this does not mean this was the main thing he wanted them to see. Such a spectacular out-of- this- world event as this draws attention to it's happening, not to Peter's issue. Jesus could have told Peter to sit down and then responded to him when he got in the boat. This would have avoided this incredible distraction, but he didn't. So Jesus must have had something more in mind other than Peter's question.

Jesus' parables are stories of events that his hearers could imagine taking place in the world they lived in. Those who heard them could relate to the people and events he describes. This is clearly not the case with this story. Humans don't walk on water in this world. So why did Jesus call Peter to walk to him on water?

The key to our understanding is realizing that Jesus was not pointing to something that would or could happen in this world. He was showing them what will be true in the new creation! *He was pointing to what we will experience when we reign with him in the kingdom of God!*

Everyone who believes in Jesus is called to follow him. We've done so and he's led us to the place of understanding. The day has dawned, the clouds are gone, and we can see clearly now.

There's Peter, walking on water to our delighted Lord. This is our next slide. Hold it before you and hear Jesus say; "Follow me, this is where we are going!" Hold it before you and imagine this as your future. This is why Jesus called Peter to walk on water. So that we can see "life after heaven." So that we can see something of what our lives will be like in the new creation.

Hold it before you and imagine a new body! A body like Jesus'! This is your body's future! Hear him say: "Follow me, this is where we are going, to your resurrection, to eternal life for your body!" The message is; "keep your eyes on me." "This is where I'm taking you." I believe the Holy Spirit led Matthew to include this story in his gospel so that we may glimpse our destiny.

Our next slide pictures Peter, with his eyes on the waves, sinking into the sea. He cries out; "Lord, save me!" Jesus takes him by the hand and lifts him out of the water saying; "You of little faith, why did you doubt?" Even in the new creation, faith, hope and love will abide. Jesus will remain our Lord. We will continue to depend on him. We will continue to follow him and do what he does. We will reach out to the nations as Jesus reached out to Peter. The Lord God will be our light and we will reign forever and ever (Revelation 22: 5).

The sea is calm in our final slide. Jesus is standing in the boat before the kneeling disciples as they worship him saying; "Truly you are the Son of God!" We've seen where we are going if we are willing to join them in worshiping and following Jesus. We've seen who we will be like. We've seen ourselves with resurrected bodies like his. We will be a light to the nations as the Lord is light to us. Along with Jesus, we will be masters of all creation. Jesus called Peter to walk on water to enable us to imagine our future.

Saint Paul would call this story a "foretaste of the gospel." It's only a foretaste, but it's enough to provide a visual illustration of our ultimate salvation! It's enough for us to imagine this incredibly glorious slice of the gospel's missing bread! In addition to hearing it, with this story the Holy Spirit enables us to picture the gospel!

The unique mission of the church is to bear witness to the gospel. Understanding the gospel requires more than just knowing the facts. The facts are past or present realities. Understanding the gospel also requires imagination. Our failure to understand the whole gospel is a failure of imagination. Understanding Holy Spirit inspired scripture requires Holy Spirit inspired imagination. Imagination enables us to envision the future. We look beyond this life into the next. Imagination gives us a glimpse into "life after heaven." A partial, inadequate, and dimily seen glimpse that falls far short of the reality yet points toward it.

Saint Paul both affirms Holy Spirit inspired imagination and acknowledges it's limits when he writes; "For now we see in a mirror, dimly, but then we will see face to face. Now I know only in part; then I will know fully, even as I have been fully known" (1 Corinthians 13: 12).

The New Testament calls the church "the bride of Christ" even more often than "the body of Christ." Revelation 21:2 reads; "And I saw the holy city, the new Jerusalem, coming down out of heaven from God, prepared as a bride adorned for her husband."

Heaven prepares us to be the bride of Christ! *When the gospel is proclaimed, The Holy Spirit is proposing to us!* He's inviting us to become members of his church, the bride of Christ. He's calling us to follow him. His proposal is found in scripture. If we accept his proposal, he vows to be with us always! He promises us an eternal world where there will be no more dying. An eternal home where sin and suffering, evil and death, have all passed away. A home where every tear is wiped away and every wound healed.

If we accept his proposal, all that Christ has will be ours! We will inherit all things with him! We will see him as he is. We will be like him in soul and body. We will be holy as he is holy. We will know all that he knows. Every question will have his answer. All truth will be ours. We will be with him wherever he goes. We will speak as he speaks and heal as he heals. We will bless the nations as Jesus has blessed us!

God loves us as he loves Jesus. If we accept his proposal, we will love each other as God loves us. His peace will cover us like a blanket.

Graditude will overflow in every heart. Every act will be filled with the joy of serving. Praise will sound from every cell of our being.

All of this and more will be ours if we accept his proposal. Trusting and obeying him leads to life after heaven. This is what life after heaven will be like. Our lives will be lived in joyous community in a glorified world! We will live as one with Jesus our bridegroom! We can only know in part what his faithfulness to his vows will mean. But we can know that "There is salvation in no one else, for there is no other name under heaven given among mortals by which we must be saved" (Acts 4: 12).

Then he said to his disciples, "The harvest is plentiful, but the laborers are few; therefore ask the Lord of the harvest to send out laborers into his harvest" (Matthew 9: 37). *Our Lord needs laborers to accept his proposal! Why not join him? No other work is as meaningful and exciting. No one else offers us heaven and life after heaven! Why would we doubt him? Why would we refuse his proposal? Why would we want to follow anyone else?*

This book has really been about love! The greatest love story ever told! God's love for us and for his creation! And even more, God's love for his Son! Our being made holy is to prepare us for the bridegroom! This is heaven's great work. This is the last slice of our missing bread. *Imagine the Father's joy when he presents a spotless bride to his only Son! Imagine the bridegroom's joy when he receives his beautiful bride! Imagine the church's joy when at last she is completely one with her bridegroom.*

There would be no joy for the Father, or the Son, or for the church, in a forced marriage! Sin enslaves but love frees. Our choice to trust Jesus makes this joy possible. It is possible because we accepted him in response to his first accepting us! It is possible because we chose to follow Jesus. Our doing so brings him joy! *Our trusting Jesus brings joy to us and joy to Jesus.*

"God is Love" is widely believed both in our churches and our culture. But God is more than love as most of us think of love. *God is Holy Love.* God is loving and holy. God is holy and loving. The two are wed together in perfect oneness. God is loving righteousness. God is pure holiness. "God is light and in him there is no darkness at all" (John 1: 5).

The bridegroom's bride will be holy as he is holy! Only a holy church is fit to be the bridegroom's bride. Our being made holy begins here and is completed in heaven! The church is the soon coming bride of Christ. When heaven's purpose is completed, Christ will return with his bride! When Christ returns,

all of heaven's saints will return with him. Then, "Blessed are the meek, for they will inherit the earth" will be realized (Matthew 5: 5).

We mean more to God than we've ever imagined. Our worth is established by our value to him. Our seeing ourselves as a member of the church, the holy bride of Christ, affords us a glimpse of our true worth. Glory to God!

"The Spirit and the bride say, "Come."

And let everyone who hears say, "Come."

And let eyerone who is thirsty Come

Let anyone who wishes take the water of life as a gift.

(Revelation 22: 17).

BIOGRAPHY

Rev. Murphy didn't plan to become a minister. After graduating with a BS in Forestry from the University of Georgia he was employed by a large paper company. He climbed the corporate ladder to a position in land management until the opportunity to purchase his grandparent's farm opened up. Five of his aunts and uncles agreed to sell and finance their undividied interest in the 910 acre farm. A bank loan enabled him to purchase cattle and begin a forestry consulting firm. The third year a second forester joined the firm as a partner.

By the time Rev. Murphy began his quest to understand how a Christian businessman should live, his farming operations and forestry enterprizes employed dozens. His beef cattle numbers had grown to 600 head on his own and leased farms. His consulting firm was managing 100,000 acres of privately owned timber land. When he left for seminary, Rev. Murphy also owned Murphy Machinery Inc. which sold and serviced logging equipment. A year earlier he'd been elected to serve on the County Board of Commissioners.

He was 33 years old when he began a serious study of the Bible. He wasn't expecting the life altering encounter that his searching brought him. His heart changing experience created a passion to be about what is truly important, helping others find our Lord. With his wife Carole and their three children, Rev. Murphy left his forestry and farming enterprises and entered seminary at Emory University in Atlanta. He sold his cattle and logging machinery dealership and left his partner the consulting business. Later they sold their home and farm. He resigned from the Board of County Commissioners when he accepted his first church his second year in seminary.

Rev. Murphy has a Master of Divinity degree from Candler School of Theology at Emory University and is an ordained Elder in the United Methodist Church. His counseling training includes a unit of Clinical Pastoral Education. He is a charter member of The American Association of Christian Counselors.

After serving a small church his last two years in seminary, Rev. Murphy was appointed to serve as an Associate Pastor at Peachtree Road United Methodist Church in Atlanta. With 4,600 members, PTRUMC was the largest United Methodist Church in the Southeast. Four years later he became the pastor of Winterville UMC near Athens, Ga. During his fourth year there, Rev. Murphy experienced a clear call to become Executive Director of Covecrest, a retreat/counseling center in the mountains of Norheast Georgia.

He and Carole invested eleven years of their lives in rescuing Covecrest financially and in building a meaningful ministry. In addition to hosting and leading retreat groups, the Murphy's began seminars teaching recovery skills to persons suffering wih panic and anxiety disorders. Later their counseling ministry included a half-way house for persons dismissed from mental health institutions. Their clients and supporters created "His Last Days," Georgia's only outdoor passion drama in 1984. The drama continues to be presented each year on Labor Day weekend at Tallulah Falls, Georgia. More information on the drama and the counseling ministry is available on their web site. When Rev. Murphy returned to the pastoral ministry, Broken Vessels Renewal Ministries a 501c3 not-for-profit cooperation was created to enable the Murphy's to continue their conseling and drama ministries.

Rev. Murphy served three more churches until his retirement from full-time ministry at age 65. He served his last church as part-time pastor for ten more years. Since retiring again, Rev. Murphy has invested much of his time in study and in writing. Rev. Murphy is a unique minister, an Evangelical Christian with an all-inclusive hope.